CU00732606

RELEVANCE THEORY

A Guide To
Successful Communication
In Translation

Ernst-August Gutt

Lectures delivered at the
Triennial Translation Workshop of UBS
Zimbabwe, 1991

Summer Institute of Linguistics
and
United Bible Societies

© 1992
Summer Institute of Linguistics, Inc.
7500 W. Camp Wisdom Road
Dallas, TX 75236
and
United Bible Societies
1865 Broadway
New York, NY 10023

ISBN 0-88312-820-9
Printed in the United States of America

CONTENTS

PREFACE

A major feature of Bible translation in the past fifty years has been its professionalization. Few Bible translators, and certainly none associated with the United Bible Societies or Wycliffe Bible Translators and the Summer Institute of Linguistics, undertake their work without some grounding in both theory and practice. Some of the most important works on theory are:

(1) *Towards a Science of Translating* by Eugene A. Nida
(2) *The Theory and Practice of Translation* by Eugene A. Nida and Charles Taber
(3) *Translating the Word of God* by John Beekman and John Callow
(4) *Bible Translation: An Introductory Course in Basic Translation Principles* by Katharine Barnwell

As theory has develc ted and practice improved, it has become obvious that there are some areas in the translation process which have not been clearly addressed by these and other writings. These include a theoretical framework to help decide which implicit material should be made explicit and certain aspects of the communication process such as irony. Ernst-August Gutt believes that part of the problem lies with the code model of communication which underlies translation theory. Consequently, he has explored the communication model known as Relevance Theory as an approach which might allow translators to handle certain of these problems more easily.

Every three years the United Bible Societies sponsor a workshop for all of their translation consultants, the purpose of which is to upgrade their professional skills and to stimulate research in translation theory. At the 1991 workshop, held at Victoria Falls in Zimbabwe from May 5–23, Dr. Gutt showed the group how Relevance Theory could serve as a successful communication model for translation. The material he shared deserves careful study, and it is for that reason that we are making his lectures available now.

Dr. Gutt is well qualified to examine the topic. His many years as a Bible translator and consultant in Ethiopia with the Summer Institute of Linguistics have given him first-hand knowledge of the problems with which translators constantly grapple. Further, his doctoral study at the University of London was under Deirdre Wilson who, along with Dan Sperber, developed relevance theory.

But it was Gutt who first saw the importance of this theory for translation.

The ultimate aim of Bible translation is to communicate as much as is possible the full interpretation of the original. I am firmly convinced that these lectures by Dr. Gutt will help us to further that aim.

Philip C. Stine

1
THE NATURE OF COMMUNICATION

I have been asked to give a series of lectures on the relevance theory of communication. There are many people who feel theory is not for them—theory is only for those inclined that way. But if one holds the view that *a theory is essentially a system of beliefs about reality*, it is difficult to think of anything more important than theory—because to live successfully in this world, it is crucial that we hold correct beliefs about it. Our beliefs should accurately represent reality.

Inadequate or wrong beliefs about reality can be dangerous. Children, for example, are not born with a system of beliefs about electricity. They need to learn that sockets are dangerous if you stick metal objects into them. If they do not hold that belief, or theory, about their surroundings, the results could be fatal. Hence, theories (i.e., our beliefs about reality) matter. The better our theories, the better adjusted we shall be to the universe in which we live.

Relevance theory is a theory of human communication. Communication is part of the world we live in, and a very important part at that; hence what we believe about communication matters. The better our beliefs agree with reality, the more successful our efforts in communication are likely to be. To take it a step further, for translation consultants (to whom these lectures are addressed and who are engaged in a rather special kind of communication, translation), the more adequate our beliefs about communication, the more successful we are likely to be in handling translations.

Therefore, I shall not apologize in any way for presenting a theoretical topic. Theory is all about our world, and we need to understand it well.

Before going into the subject matter, let me give you some idea of where we are going. The first lecture will deal with the nature of communication and then bring out a couple of implications for some fairly common assumptions about translation. The basic structure of each lecture will follow the same pattern, first introducing some insights of relevance theory and then bringing out some of the consequences for us as translators. The second lecture will deal with the heart of relevance theory: the principle of relevance. The third lecture will show that relevance theory comes with a ready-made notion of faithfulness. In the fourth lecture we shall see how relevance theory accounts for various nonliteral uses of language, including poetic uses. In the final lecture we shall try to pull everything together by trying to understand the requirements for successful translation and their implications for the decision-making process in translating.

I shall follow the convention of referring to the communicator in the abstract as "she" and to the addressee as "he" as Sperber and Wilson do in their book (1986a) and some of their other works. This convention makes the discussion clearer and the presentation easier. In addition, it seems particularly appropriate at a workshop where feminist concerns are given special attention. (I have no evidence that Sperber and Wilson's strategy was intended to imply that one of the two sexes is more dominant in communication.)

1.1 Inference

Situation 1. A few weeks ago we had a family holiday at Lake Langano in Ethiopia, one of the Rift Valley lakes. One afternoon I watched the opposite shore, perhaps ten kilometers away, grow darker. Rain could be seen coming down, and before too long a grey curtain hid the opposite shore line. I said to myself, "It looks as if we are going to get rain here before too long."

Situation 2. Before going on that holiday, things looked rather unstable in Ethiopia. Late on Sunday evening the colleague who was to look after our responsibilities while I was on holiday rang and asked if we could discuss the situation before I left. I asked if we could do that early in the morning. He answered, "I need to be at the university really early." I knew that he did not think we could meet early that morning.

Situation 3. In March I was on business in Nairobi. As I was walking to church, I saw two African ladies. One was wearing an Ethiopian dress. As they were passing by, I heard one say to the other, "*Awo, sira agignt^wal,*" an Amharic sentence meaning, "Yes, he has found work." I said to myself, "Aha, these are two Ethiopian ladies."

Three examples—of what? In one case, I observed a natural phenomenon, and that observation gave rise to thoughts that went beyond what I saw. In the second case, I was given an utterance, and it gave rise to a thought not expressed by that utterance. In the third case, I came to a fairly firm conclusion about the country of origin of some total strangers, without anybody telling me anything about them.

How did these thoughts come about? The most natural explanation is *inference*: I combined what I saw and heard with knowledge

I already possessed and arrived at conclusions not obtained from the observation nor from my previous knowledge alone.

The thought processes could have been something like the following: I had observed many times that when it started raining on the opposite shore, it would not take long before the rain reached our shore. In other words, over a period of time I had developed the belief that when there is rain on the opposite shore, it is very likely to spread quickly to our shore. There was rain on the opposite shore in the afternoon of Tuesday, April 9th. Therefore it was likely that there would be rain on our shore on the afternoon of that day. We can represent this simple inference by the following argument (details aside):

Premise 1: When there is rain on the opposite shore, it is very likely to spread quickly to our shore. (prior knowledge)

Premise 2: There was rain on the opposite shore on the afternoon of Tuesday, April 9th. (information available from observation)

Conclusion: Therefore, it was likely that there would be rain on our shore on the afternoon of that day.

The second example works the same way. You have to know that our home is not near the university. Therefore, if my colleague planned to be at the university early, he could not meet me early.

Premise 1: If my colleague wanted to be at the university early, he could not meet me early. (prior knowledge)

Premise 2: My colleague wanted to be at the university early. (information obtained from utterance)

Conclusion: Therefore, my colleague could not meet me early.

The third example is a little more involved in that there are two independent arguments involved.

ARGUMENT 1

Premise 1: An African lady wearing an Ethiopian dress is likely to be Ethiopian. (prior knowledge)

Premise 2: The lady I saw wore an Ethiopian dress.

Conclusion: Therefore, the lady was likely to be Ethiopian.

ARGUMENT 2

Premise 1: A person speaking Amharic is likely to be Ethiopian.

Premise 2: The person I saw was speaking Amharic.

Conclusion: Therefore, the person I saw was likely to be Ethiopian.

In this third example, I arrived at the same conclusion by two independent lines of evidence, which made that conclusion stronger than if I had had only one line of evidence, for example, if I had only seen the lady wearing an Ethiopian dress without hearing her speak Amharic. Note that the content of the utterance was of no consequence to my conclusion; all that figured for me was the fact that the utterance was in Amharic.

Details aside, I do not think that these examples are particularly controversial. However, they do bear witness to some rather consequential facts: First, *our beliefs have inferential properties*, allowing us to arrive at new (true) beliefs on the basis of "old" true beliefs. And this is what inference really is: Inference is a truth-preserving logical operation.

Second, *we make frequent use of inferential processes in our daily lives*, without even being aware of this fact.

Third, *we use inference to interpret verbal communication as well as other experiences*. Thus, in the second situation inference was crucial to arrive at the interpretation intended by my colleague: He was not just telling me that he needed to be at the university early—he was trying to tell me that he would not be able to meet me at the proposed time, and why not.

1.2 The code model and semiotics

Obvious as these insights may seem, the fact that inference plays a central role in human communication has been largely overlooked until quite recently. In fact, the most common and most basic assumption about human communication has been that it works by *encoding and decoding*. We have a thought, or "message," in our head; we use the rules of a natural language—English, German—to encode this message in a sign or signal, that is, in spoken or written words; we use a medium or channel to transfer it, that is, acoustically or visually. Then the receptor receives the signal and reverses the coding processes: applying the rules of the language to the signal, he or she arrives at the message.

This idea of signs encoding some message or meaning was then extended, to include, for example, the whole of culture. Thus Leach made the following proposal:

> I shall assume that *all* the various non-verbal dimensions of culture, such as style in clothing, village lay-out, architecture, furniture, food, cooking, music, physical gestures, postural attitudes and so on are organised in patterned sets so as to incorporate coded information in a manner analogous to the sounds and words and sentences of a natural language. I

assume therefore it is just as meaningful to talk about the grammatical rules which govern the wearing of clothes as it is to talk about the grammatical rules which govern speech utterances. (Leach 1976:10)

The general framework of *semiotics* (Peirce) and *semiology* (Saussure) was developed in this way.

In the framework of semiotics, my idea that the lady wearing an Ethiopian dress was Ethiopian would have been seen as a process not of inference, but of decoding: the wearing of Ethiopian clothes is a cultural signal that encodes that the person is an Ethiopian. (Of course, it would be possible for someone to misuse the code in various ways.)

Now in order to avoid any serious misunderstanding, let me stress at this point that there is no doubt whatsoever that encoding and decoding *can* and very often *do* play a role in human communication. Natural languages in particular usually do involve coding relationships. So relevance theory does not claim that communication necessarily works without coding.

Nevertheless, there are serious problems with the view that communication *consists in* the encoding and decoding of messages. The main reason for these reservations is that there are many aspects of human communication for which the code model simply cannot account.

Let us start with our second example, where my colleague told me, "I need to be at the university really early," and I understood him as saying that he could not meet me early that morning. If the code model of communication were correct, then there must be rules which decode from the string of signs of the English language "I need to be at the university really early" the message "I cannot meet you early."

Of course, we could simply assume that such a rule exists: "I need to be at the university really early" *means* "I cannot meet you early."

But suppose my colleague's wife had asked him that same evening if she could have the car in the morning, and he had used the same sentence in reply, meaning that she could not have the car in the morning. Again, if the code model were correct, then there should be another rule to the effect that "I need to be at the university really early" is to be decoded as "You cannot have the car in the morning."

It is easy to see that this approach cannot be the right one. For one thing, we could easily go on constructing new messages which this sentence could be used to convey, making the code of English more and more complicated. Secondly, and more significantly, serious questions about the adequacy of the code model would arise already at the point where there were two possible messages that could be conveyed by the same string of signs. The code model can possibly explain how the different possible messages could be decoded, but what means would it have for deciding which of the possible messages was the one intended on a given occasion of utterance?

The obvious answer seems to be to refer to *context*—the context would disambiguate the utterance. While it is undoubtedly true that context helps to disambiguate utterances, it is by no means clear how this could be explained in the code model framework. It seems the best that model could do would be to add more and more rules for decoding that made reference to contextual factors. For example, the sentence "I need to be at the university really early" means "I cannot meet you early in the morning" if used in answer to the question "Can I meet you early in the morning?" However, this rule would not be adequate alone. Suppose that my colleague and I usually met at the university. In that case the sentence "I need to be at the university really early" would be understood as an assent to the proposal: "Yes, let's meet early next morning since I need to be there early anyway." So the contextual factors would have to be spelled out more explicitly in the decoding rules. It is not difficult to see that this strategy would result in an *immensely complicated code*, raising the question whether it is psychologically plausible to assume that such a complex system could ever be acquired.

Another basic problem with the code model view is that the information linguistically encoded in a sentence seriously underdetermines the intended meaning. Suppose I get a phone call and my wife asks me after I put down the receiver, "Who was it?" I reply, "Oh, it was Phil." Now there are a number of individuals called "Phil" that both my wife and I know, but the linguistic form of my utterance does not tell that it was Phil Stine I had in mind. Thus the linguistic form does not specify a proposition that could be true or false. Further information is needed to develop the linguistically specified skeleton into a full proposition.

Another example (given by Sperber and Wilson 1986a:189) concerns time. Compare the following two utterances:

(a) have had breakfast.
(b) have been to Tibet.

While it would be appropriate to use the second utterance even if your visit to Tibet was as far back as ten years, it would be felt to be inappropriate to use the first utterance if the last breakfast you had was two or three days back. Again, there is no clue in the linguistically coded form that would indicate that different time scales are being thought about. This information is supplied extralinguistically, from what we know about having meals and about traveling. As Sperber and Wilson (1986a) point out, the semantic representations of sentences provide only incomplete schemas that need to be developed further into fully specified assumptions with the help of contextual information.

Many other instances of communication could be adduced that seem to pose serious problems to the code model—irony, for example, and so-called weak communication or vagueness. However, let me give an example from Sperber and Wilson (1986a) that shows very nicely that a message can be communicated even in violation of an unambiguously defined and agreed code:

> In the Stalin era, two friends in the West were arguing. Paul had decided to emigrate to Russia, which he saw as a land of justice and freedom. He would go and write back to Henry to let him know the beautiful truth. Henry tried to persuade him not to go: there was oppression and misery in Russia, he claimed, goods were scarce, and Paul's letters would be censored anyhow. Since Paul would not be moved, Henry persuaded him to accept at least the following convention: if Paul wrote back in black ink, Henry would know he was sincere. If he wrote in purple ink, Henry would understand that Paul was not free to report the truth. Six months after Paul's departure, Henry received the following letter, written in black ink: "Dear Henry, this is the country of justice and freedom. It is a worker's paradise. In the shops you can find everything you need, with the sole exception of purple ink . . ." (p. 170)

As Sperber and Wilson argue, ". . . the coded signal, even if it is ambiguous, is only a piece of evidence about the communicator's intentions, and has to be used inferentially and in a context" (p. 170). Thus inference can override coding, and hence is the more basic factor in communication.

1.3 Inferential communication

How, then, according to relevance theory, does human communication work in the most basic terms? The communicator has some thoughts that she wants the audience to recognize. She tries to achieve this by showing some kind of behavior—that is, by producing some kind of *stimulus*—from which the audience can *infer* two things:

(1) the fact that the communicator intends to communicate something to the audience (this is called the *communicative intention*)

(2) what it is that the communicator intends to communicate (this is called the *informative intention* of the communicator and can be thought of as a set of *of assumptions*)

Communication that involves these two elements—a communicative intention as well as an informative intention—is called *ostensive-inferential communication.* It is this kind of communication that Sperber and Wilson concentrate on. There are other kinds of communication (e.g., information processing in machines), but they work rather differently, and it seems true to say that the bulk of human communication is *ostensive-inferential.*

When is an act of communication successful? When the audience succeeds in inferring the informative intention of the communicator.

What is necessary for achieving this? From the point of view of the communicator, she faces a twofold challenge. She must find or produce a stimulus that will fulfil two requirements: It must (1) make clear to the audience that she wants to communicate, and (2) have the right properties to help them draw those inferences that she intends to convey rather than any other inferences.

From the point of view of the addressee, he must derive from the stimulus those inferences which the communicator intended him to draw.

How does this approach to communication relate to coding? The stimulus used to convey the communicator's intentions *can*, of course, make use of a code. The use of language does this. However, coding as such is neither a necessary nor a sufficient condition for human communication to take place: It is not *necessary* because a lot of human communication happens without coding or, as we just saw, even overrides the code; it is not *sufficient* because inference needs to take place as well.

1.4 Implications for translation

What about *translation?* As you are probably aware, the most explicit accounts of translation that we have had so far rely on the code model of communication—either explicitly or implicitly. To the degree that the code model is inadequate, we can also expect code-model-based views of translation to be inadequate. Or, to express things more positively, to the degree that the inferential theory of communication overcomes inadequacies in the code model of communication, we can also expect better insights into the nature of translation.

It will be the aim of the following lectures to substantiate this claim. However, let me first give you a little preview of the sort of difference that the application of relevance theory can make to our work as translators and translation consultants.

1.4.1 Benefits of relevance theory: a sharper tool for exegesis

Relevance theory provides a *much sharper tool for meaning analysis, or exegesis,* than the code model. Consequently it can lead to a much deeper understanding of the meaning of the original text. An example of this benefit can be seen in the following analysis of John 14:28, "If you loved me, you would be glad that I am going to the Father, for the Father is greater than I."

A kind of structural semantic analysis (based on a code model approach) of John 14:28 would run something like this:

(1) If you loved me (expresses a condition for the thought expressed in clause 2)

(2) you would be glad that I am going to the Father (expresses the consequence of the condition stated in clause 1 and also states the result of the reason expressed in clause 3)

(3) for the Father is greater than I. (expresses the reason for the thought expressed in clauses 1 and 2 taken together)

Thus, in this structural analysis, we have identified the relationships between the thoughts expressed in the three clauses by assigning certain relational labels to them. There may be some quibbles about the most appropriate labels to use (e.g., whether the relation between 2 and 3 should be called effect and cause rather than result and reason), but essentially the work is done once the labels have been assigned.

Yet even after we have done this analysis, we may still feel uneasy: What is Jesus actually trying to say in this sentence? Why would the disciples, if they loved Jesus, be glad that he is going to the Father? And how does the fact that the Father is greater than Jesus enter into that? Thus there remain questions that need to be answered if we are to really understand the meaning of this text. But the structural analysis does not even raise these questions, let alone answer them.

The inferential approach on which relevance theory is based works rather differently. For example, the conjunction *if*, which is essentially a processing instruction that tells us what to do with the proposition it marks, would tell us that the proposition introduced by *if* is to be treated as a premise in an argument, where the truth of that premise is not asserted. This can be applied to the verse we just looked at. The presence of *if* between the first and second clause of the sentence guides the hearer to construct an inferential argument that has at least the following elements:

Premise 1: if the disciples loved Jesus (contrafactual)
Conclusion: the disciples would be glad that Jesus was going to the Father.

Clearly this argument is incomplete. Without further premises the conclusion does not follow, and a real understanding of this part of the utterance requires a completion of the argument. In other words, by expressing himself in this way, Jesus intends the audience to supply further premises, so that a valid inference results. Without these further premises, the utterance remains obscure.

One fairly obvious way of completing this argument would be to supply the following further assumptions:

If you love someone, you are glad when something good happens to that person. Going to the Father would be good for Jesus.

This would yield the following argument:

Premise 1: If you love someone, you are glad when something good happens to that person.
Premise 2: If the disciples loved Jesus, they would be glad when something good happens to him.
Premise 3: Going to the Father would be good for Jesus.
Conclusion: The disciples would be glad that Jesus was going to the Father.

This would be a possible analysis, and it would answer at least one of the points we felt uneasy about earlier on: If the disciples loved Jesus, why should they be glad about his going to God the Father?

However, Jesus added a third clause, marking it by *for*. In relevance-theoretic terms, *for* again encodes a processing instruction. It instructs the hearer to treat the thought expressed as a premise in an argument and, furthermore, as a premise that is assumed to be true. (Note that while *if* also introduces a premise in an argument, it does not automatically entitle the audience to treat it as true.) Thus the skeleton of the argument that Jesus wants us to construct has not only one, but at least two premises:

Premise 1:   if the disciples loved Jesus (contrafactual)
Premise n: for the Father is greater than I
Conclusion: the disciples would be glad that Jesus was going to the Father.

Again, Jesus expected his audience to supply further information to understand his point. What could this further information have been? Since our main concern here is one of principle rather than exegetical detail, we shall not take the time to dig deeper into this passage. (You may want to do that at your leisure.)

For now, let me just briefly point out that one important consideration for relevance theory in general is that the *accessibility* of information to be supplied plays an important role. In other words, the more reason there is to believe that a particular piece of information was easily accessible to the hearers, the more likely it is to be the right (i.e., speaker-intended) piece of information—other things being equal. (We'll hear more about those "other things" later on.)

Thus, the inferential approach is superior to a code-based approach in that it encourages the analyst to penetrate to the level of the actual thought processes in order to get a proper understanding of the text. In the inferential model, labeling relationships is not enough. We must also try to understand the thoughts behind those relationships.

It is not difficult to see that this is very useful to help not only the translator but also the *consultant* gain a much more thorough understanding of the text. It enables the consultant to bring out into the open what assumptions go into particular interpretations of a passage and to examine and evaluate them objectively.

1.4.2 Benefits of relevance theory: a tool for understanding translation problems

Another benefit of the inferential approach to communication is that it can help us toward *a more adequate understanding of translation problems*. Hence, it can also help us to arrive at better solutions.

In the code model, transmission of the right message depends primarily on correct coding: If the message is encoded and decoded correctly, then communication should succeed. There is, of course, the possibility of disturbance by "noise" in the channel. But if a message is encoded correctly and decoded correctly, and if there is no disturbance by noise, the code model would predict the success of the communication act.

However, this prediction is not correct as seen in the following example:

(a) Margaret: Could you have a quick look at my printer—it's not working right.
(b) Mike: I have an appointment at eleven o'clock.

The meaning encoded by Mike's reply is clear: at eleven o'clock he has an appointment with somebody. (Note that to understand even this, nonlinguistic information needs to be used.) However, the coded meaning by itself gives no clue as to what his answer to the question actually is, that is, what message he intends to convey, since the information expressed in the utterance needs to be processed inferentially in order to recover the intended meaning. For example, suppose it is five minutes to eleven. Margaret, being aware that printer problems usually cannot be solved in a couple of minutes, would understand the intended message to be negative—Mike has no time to look at the printer now.

On the other hand, if the time were a quarter past ten, Mike's answer would probably be taken to mean "I have a limited amount of time to look at the printer now," with the further implication that this may not be enough time to solve the problem.

Thus, though the meaning encoded is the same on both occasions, the utterance would give a very different message in each case. The code model does not make this prediction.

This failure to recognize the inferential nature of communication has had far-reaching consequences in translation. For one thing, it has led to the belief that the main problem in translation is finding the right target-language expression for the meaning intended in the source language; it is assumed that correct encoding will ensure correct understanding. However, just as identity in encoded meaning of two expressions of the *same* language does not guarantee identity of the message conveyed by them, neither does identity in encoded meaning of two expressions of *different* languages guarantee identity of the message conveyed. Even a correctly encoded message can be seriously misunderstood.

By suggesting that successful communication depends primarily on correct coding, the code model has given rise to the tendency to assume that miscommunication in translation results from incorrect encoding, that is, from a translation mistake. On the inferential model, however, miscommunication is not nearly as directly linked to inappropriate use of the linguistic code: it is as likely to result from wrong inference, especially from the use of unintended premises.

Let me illustrate this with an example from "Ruth in Central Africa: A Cultural Commentary," a chapter in Ernst Wendland's 1987 book, with which most of you will be familiar. As you will recall, this provides examples of misinterpretations of the book of Ruth that are likely to arise in a Central African context. One of these instances refers to the timing of Ruth's return to her home town: "So Naomi returned from Moab . . . , arriving in Bethlehem as the barley harvest was beginning" (Ruth 1:22, NIV).

Wendland comments:

> The time reference here is important, since in a Tonga sociocultural setting it would immediately arouse the suspicions of the people whose village Naomi was entering. A person does not usually move during the period extending from after the fields have been planted until after the harvest has been completed. One's crops mean life, and therefore it must have been some serious offense which drove Naomi away from her former home at such a time. Perhaps it had been that she was guilty of practising witchcraft—after all, were not all her men now dead? (p. 171)

The problem here is not that the translation expresses the wrong meaning. Rather, *the events themselves* that are reported to have happened lead the audience to draw wrong inferences due to culturally conditioned premises. (To make matters worse, several points of the story seem to reinforce these wrong inferences.) Thus we see that encoding the right meaning does not guarantee communicative success, and that miscommunication is not necessarily due to wrong encoded meaning.

Translation theories that automatically assume that the cause of miscommunication is mistranslation not only run into serious difficulties, but are also a source of considerable frustration to translators. We shall return to this later. But for now, let me briefly summarize the main points of this lecture.

1.5 Summary

Inference is fundamental to human communication: the communicator produces a stimulus from which the audience can infer that she intends to communicate something and what it is that she intends to convey. The stimulus may make use of a code, but the existence or use of a code is neither a necessary nor a sufficient condition for communication to take place.

The inferential approach of relevance theory allows us to penetrate to a deeper and more precise level of understanding texts than the code model does. Reliance on the code model has led to inadequate assumptions in translation. One such assumption is that correct encoding in the target language leads to correct understanding and that therefore the communication of wrong meaning points to a faulty translation.

The next lecture will focus on the question of how the audience manages to draw the correct (i.e., communicator-intended) inferences from the stimulus. This will lead us to relevance theory and the centerpiece of the theory—the principle of relevance.

2
THE PRINCIPLE OF RELEVANCE

2.1 Recapitulation

In the first lecture we saw that communication works inferentially: The communicator produces a stimulus from which the audience infers the thoughts she intends to communicate. Coding may or may not be involved.

But, of course, there are innumerable inferences one can draw from any stimulus. For example, the lady at the check-in desk of an airline might greet you in a hoarse voice, "Good morning, sir. May I have your ticket please?" From this verbal stimulus you can draw any number of inferences: that the lady can speak, that she speaks English, that she has caught a cold, that she has seen you, that she is being polite, that she knows what time of day it is, that she wants to see your ticket, and so forth. So there is obviously a need for some constraint that will enable the audience to know which inferences are the intended ones.

2.2 Relevance

The crucial notion that enables people to know which inferences the communicator intended is *relevance*. What is relevance? For an utterance to be relevant, it needs not only to be *new* (in some sense), but it must also link up with the *context* in some way.

The water in Lake Langano is a light brown color and there are lots of catfish in the lake. While the information contained in this utterance will be new for most of you, it does not seem relevant, since it does not connect to anything I have just said. (Of course, this last remark shows that this utterance is, in fact, relevant after all: it serves as illustration of a point I just made.)

The technical notion by which relevance theory captures the link-up between an utterance and its context is called *contextual effect:* in order to be perceived as relevant, an utterance must have contextual effects.

Before we pursue this matter of relevance and contextual effects further, we need to clarify what we mean by *context*, which is a word used with different meaning by different people. In relevance theory, context is understood as "the set of premises used in interpreting an utterance" (Sperber and Wilson 1986a:15). As such, it is, in relevance theory, a *psychological notion:* it refers to a subset of the hearer's belief about the world—more precisely it refers to a part of the *cognitive environment* of the hearer.

The cognitive environment is a very comprehensive notion: the cognitive environment of an individual consists of all the facts that that individual is capable of representing in his mind and of accepting as true, or probably true. The sources of this information can be *perception* (seeing, hearing, etc.) *memory*, or *inference*, which can make use of information from the other two sources.

The notion of context in relevance theory is very rich.

> A context in this sense is not limited to information about the immediate physical environment or the immediately preceding utterances: expectations about the future, scientific hypotheses or religious beliefs, anecdotal memories, general cultural assumptions, beliefs about the mental state of the speaker, may all play a role in interpretation. (Sperber and Wilson 1986a:15–16)

With this clarification, let us now return to the link-up itself between what is said and the context. Remember, relevance theory defines this link-up in terms of *contextual effects*.

A contextual effect is a modification of one's cognitive environment that could not have been achieved by the stimulus alone, nor by the context alone, but only by the inferential combination of *both.*

To see this, let us return to the second of the situations described at the beginning of section 1.1 in the first lecture.

Premise 1: If my colleague wanted to be at the university early, he could not meet me early. (prior knowledge)
Premise 2: My colleague wanted to be at the university early. (information obtained from utterance)
Conclusion: My colleague could not meet me early.

Premise 1 of this argument is part of my prior knowledge: in relevance-theoretic terms, it is a *contextual assumption.* Premise 2 of the argument is expressed by the utterance itself, and it is relevant in the context of premise 1 because it yields the conclusion "My colleague could not meet me early" as a contextual effect. This thought is a genuine contextual effect since it follows neither from the contextual assumption alone, nor from the utterance alone, but from the inferential combination of the two.

As Sperber and Wilson (1986a:109) point out, there are three kinds of contextual effects that make for relevance:

– derivation of a contextual implication

 – strengthening of a contextual assumption
 – elimination of a contextual assumption through contradiction

The example just looked at illustrates the *derivation of a contextual implication:* The conclusion is an implication of the stimulus and a contextual assumption.

The idea of *contextual strengthening* is based on the fact that we do not hold all beliefs with equal strength. Thus while I am firmly convinced that there is water in the Atlantic Ocean, I am much less certain that I will be able to visit Victoria Falls again. As Sperber and Wilson (1986a:77) point out, the strength with which we hold a belief depends on two things: the way in which we arrived at the thought, and its relation to other beliefs we hold. We tend to give high credibility to information obtained from perception—for example, from what we see.

On the other hand, a belief can be strengthened if it is inferentially supported by other beliefs. This is seen in regard to the third situation described at the beginning of section 1.1 about a lady in Ethiopian dress. My assumption that she was Ethiopian was much stronger when a second piece of evidence became available that was logically independent of the first observation, that is, when I noticed that the lady spoke Amharic.

The following text illustrates the case of the strengthening of a contextual assumption in communication:

(a) Christine is really clever.
(b) She has an average of 98% in maths.

Here the claim expressed by utterance (a) forms part of the context for utterance (b). What is the contextual effect of utterance (b)? A further assumption, readily accessible through the notion of cleverness and achievements in maths, would be the following:

A person with an average of 98% in maths is clever.

Combined with this contextual assumption, utterance (b) yields the contextual assumption (a) as an inference:

(a) A person with an average of 98% in maths is clever.
(b) Christine has an average of 98% in maths.
(c) Christine is clever.

As a result, the contextual assumption "Christine is really clever" is not just a claim, but is inferentially strengthened by further evidence.

The notion of the *elimination of a contextual assumption* can again be illustrated from the second situation in section 1.1. As you may recall, my initial question was whether we could meet early the next morning, to which my colleague replied, "I need to be at the university really early." This initial question constituted a contextual assumption for the remainder of the conversation. As we saw, my colleague's reply yielded the contextual implication "My colleague could not meet me early," and this contextual implication in turn cancelled the contextual assumption expressed by my question.

So contextual effects make for relevance, and the more contextual effects an utterance achieves with an audience, the more relevant it will be to that audience.

However, very little in life is for free, and contextual effects are no exception. Processing an utterance requires *mental effort*—for the linguistic decoding, for the inferential processes, and for retrieving information from memory. Sperber and Wilson (1986a:124–25) claim that relevance is dependent not only on contextual effects, but is also sensitive to processing cost, in that the more effort the processing of a stimulus requires, the less relevant it is felt to be. Thus, relevance is seen as the *cost-benefit* relation of processing effort spent versus contextual effects obtained.

2.3 The principle of relevance

As we consider how relevance helps communication, here is where the fact that we are dealing with ostensive communication becomes important. As you may recall from the first lecture, in ostensive communication the communicator makes clear to the audience that she has a communicative intention. That is, *she claims the attention* of the audience, indicating that she intends to convey some thoughts to the audience. By doing so, she tacitly communicates her belief that the information she has to offer will be worth the audience's while, or in terms of relevance theory, that it will be relevant to the audience.

To be more precise, the tacit claim inherent in ostensive communication is not only that the information she has to offer is relevant to the audience, but that it is *optimally relevant*, optimal relevance being defined as follows:

(a) The set of assumptions which the communicator intends to make manifest to the addressee is relevant enough to make it worth the addressee's while to process the ostensive stimulus.

(b) The ostensive stimulus is the most relevant one the communicator could have used to communicate that set of assumptions. (Sperber and Wilson 1986a:158)

Note that the claims that this definition makes are different on the benefit side and on the cost side. On the benefit side (i.e., concerning the relevance of the information offered), the claim is one of *adequacy* (i.e., under optimal processing there will be adequate contextual effects for the audience). Incidentally, there is no fixed level of relevance that all utterances are supposed to achieve. A casual remark about the weather offered to a fellow commuter at a bus stop is likely to achieve a much lower degree of relevance than a sentence in the abstract of a scientific paper.

On the cost side, the claim is one of *minimal effort*. In order to have her informative intention recognized, it is in the interest of the communicator to make this task as easy as possible for the audience.

This psychological fact about ostensive communication is captured in the *principle of relevance*, which is that "every act of ostensive-inferential communication communicates the presumption of its own optimal relevance" (Sperber and Wilson 1986a:158). In other words, whenever a person engages in ostensive communication, she creates the tacit presumption that what she has to communicate will be optimally relevant to the audience: that it will yield adequate contextual effects, without requiring unnecessary processing effort.

The central importance of this principle is that it has the effect of *singling out the intended interpretation for the audience*. It entitles the audience to assume that the first interpretation which has adequate contextual effects and which did not cause the audience unnecessary processing effort must be the one intended by the communicator. That is, *the first interpretation found to be consistent with the principle of relevance must be the intended interpretation*—for reasons of relevance, no other interpretation needs to be considered.

In fact, since we cannot read each other's thoughts, consistency with the principle of relevance is the *only* criterion audiences have to arrive at the speaker-intended interpretation of an utterance. There is no other way. As we shall see, this claim has very important implications for translators.

This may be a good point at which to emphasize that the principle of relevance works subconsciously and automatically. It is not some constraint we have learned that may or may not apply. It is rather a basic fact of our human psychology, probably a particular application of a much more general innate optimization constraint. In fact, while we do have intuitions about relevance, we have no awareness of the mental processes by which it is established in our minds.

To see how the principle of relevance guides the audience to the intended interpretation, let us see how it applies to the previously mentioned second situation in section 1.1. The utterance we want to deal with is the reply: "I need to be at the university really early." What is the intended interpretation of this stimulus likely to be?

When presented with this ostensive stimulus, the psychological fact of the principle of relevance leads the audience to expect adequate benefits from it, that is, adequate contextual effects. But contextual effects arise only in a context. What is this context?

Again, the expectation of optimal relevance leads the audience to start with highly accessible information first. In a continuous conversation, such as we have here, the most highly accessible contextual information is that given by the immediately preceding utterance. Thus the initial context for interpreting this utterance is the question: "Can we meet early tomorrow morning?" So, if I am on the right track with my interpretation, my colleague's answer will yield at least some contextual effects with this question as context.

Furthermore, the occurrence of *university* makes accessible all kinds of information I know about the university, including the knowledge that the university is quite far from our home, so that it would be impossible for him to be early at the university and meet me early in the morning. This realization would be another contextual assumption, which may be represented as follows:

If he needs to be at the university early, then he cannot meet me early.

Taking this contextual assumption together with the utterance, we get the following inference:

(a) *Thought expressed by utterance:* He needs to be at the university really early.
(b) *Contextual assumption:* If he needs to be at the university early, then he cannot meet me early.
(c) *Contextual implication:* He cannot meet me early.
(d) *Contextual assumption:* He can meet me at the university early (truth unknown).
(e) Cancellation of contextual assumption (d).

Thus, contextual implication (c) cancels the proposition (d) expressed in my earlier question whether we could meet early at the university. Hence, it has the further contextual effect of eliminating a wrong contextual assumption.

This example gives some idea of how contextual effects can interact and build on each other in complex ways as a text unfolds. It suggests that propositional displays of "semantic structure" are likely to be too simplistic to be adequate. The utterance does lead to contextual effects. (Adequacy would depend on the situation.)

What about the processing cost? Note that we used only highly accessible contextual information—that which was expressed in the *preceding* utterance along with contextual information associated with one of the concepts referred to in the utterance itself. Therefore this interpretation did not involve unnecessary processing.

Consequently, the interpretation arrived at satisfies the condition of consistency with the principle of relevance. This explains our intuition that this is the intended interpretation.

Thus, the way the principle of relevance facilitates communication is by causing stimulus, context, and interpretation to interact inferentially: Constrained by the principle of relevance, the inferential combination of stimulus and context will lead to the intended interpretation.

2.4 Secondary communication situations and communicability

One of the problems of translating Scripture is that it involves the presentation of texts written for one audience to another audience with a different background. In relevance-theoretic terms, this means that one attempts to communicate a given informative intention to an audience other than the one for which this information was meant in the first place. I refer to such instances as *secondary communication situations.*

We have already illustrated how the same stimulus can lead to rather different contextual effects when processed in different contexts. A clear example of this was the way in which the story of Ruth was misinterpreted in the context brought to it by the Tonga people. Secondary communication situations are, in fact, likely to result in miscommunication.

Secondary communication situations can have even more damaging effects than that. They may lead to a total breakdown of communication.

For example, all of us who are translation consultants have moved and are still moving in cultures not our own. Even if we have learned a local language or can use some lingua franca, all of us have experienced the puzzles of a cross-cultural communication situation. For example, looking at it from the hearer's end, when somebody talks to us, we understand perfectly well what the person is saying as far as the linguistic content of the utterance is concerned, and yet we may not be clear at all as to what the person is driving at with her utterance. Looking at it from the communicator's end, we all know or can think of certain things that we cannot communicate to certain people because they lack the necessary background.

Within the relevance-theoretic framework these problems are only what one would expect. Miscommunication in secondary communication situations follows from the fact that the interdependence of stimulus, context, and interpretation is *inferential*. Generally speaking, the validity of an inferential argument depends on its premises; if different premises are supplied, the original conclusion may no longer follow. Likewise, if the new context is so different that no adequate contextual effects are achieved, the audience will be at a loss to know what the communicator was trying to get across.

Thus we see that our inferential account of communication entails a *condition of communicability:* An intended interpretation is recoverable not in just any context, but *only in a context where the requirements of optimal processing are fulfilled,* that is, where there are adequate contextual effects, without unnecessary processing effort. If the audience fails to arrive at an interpretation that satisfies these conditions, it has no means of finding the intended interpretation. In fact, successful communication requires that the utterance be processed in the context envisaged by the communicator.

This fact is not explained or predicted by the code model of communication. As long as the code is adequate and there is no "noise" in the channel, any message ought to be communicable to anybody. Accordingly, scholars have tended to debate the question of effability—the claim that each proposition or thought is expressible by some sentence in every language—and the closely related question of translatability. But the question of communicability, which seems more fundamental, has found little attention.

This condition of communicability, which is a psychological one, is of great significance for translation. Many problems encountered in translation involve violations of this condition.

Such a problem was encountered by Thomas Headland (1981) among the Casiguran Dumagat, a Negrito society of hunter-gatherers, living in a tropical rain forest in the Philippines. Headland found that there seemed to be a serious information overload in the Greek text for the Dumagat people. As he is careful to explain, the problem was not that the information was given at too high a *rate*, but rather that the actual *amount* of information was too much. For example, Luke reports how Paul first met Aquila and Priscilla in Acts 18:2 as follows:

> There he met a Jew named Aquila, a native of Pontus, who had recently come from Italy with his wife Priscilla, because Claudius had ordered all the Jews to leave Rome. (NIV)

This statement provides quite a bit of information in addition to the fact that Paul met these two people. To Headland the problem was not that all this information is expressed in one sentence; even when divided into several sentences, there was simply *too much* information for the Dumagat. All they would be interested in was something like "There he met a Jew named Aquila and his wife Priscilla."

Headland proposes that this may be due to a difference in the ways Dumagats think as compared to Greeks. Relevance theory, however, offers a rather simple explanation of this phenomenon: given that the Dumagat people have no knowledge of the geography of the Roman Empire at the time of Paul, the mention of Pontus, Italy, or Rome has no significance whatsoever for them. Furthermore, since they are totally unfamiliar with the political situation of the time, the fact that Claudius had ordered all Jews to leave Rome would again be of little, if any, relevance to them. In terms of relevance, the text requires them to process a fair bit of unfamiliar information that would yield very few, if any, contextual effects for them. On the recognition that adequate contextual effects are a precondition for successful communication, it is hardly surprising that the Dumagat people stalled.

Headland (1981:19) reports further that this problem was not limited to a few isolated verses, but to longer passages as well, where the Dumagat people simply did not seem to get the point:

> I am fairly sure that no Dumagat believer has yet grasped the important significance of the first church council in Jerusalem, as reported in Acts 15. Luke would be more than disappointed to see how the Dumagat misses the point . . . There must be a way too, I suppose, to get the message of Hebrews 7 across, that the reason that Jesus is a better intervener for us to God than the Levitical priests is because Abraham gave tithes to Melchizedek! That message ought to get across—it is the central message of that section of the book. Why don't the Dumagat readers get it?

While I am not sufficiently familiar with the Dumagat situation to give a definitive analysis, it seems more than likely that the difference in contextual knowledge between first-century Greeks and present day Dumagat is such that communicability would be seriously affected.

Against this background, it comes as no surprise at all that receptors are often not very interested in biblical texts, a problem that is being recognized more and more clearly, sometimes referred to as that of "Scripture use." If relevance theory is right at all, one of the critical conditions on which successful communication depends is that there must be adequate contextual effects. If the context which the receptors bring to the translated text is so different that there are few or even no contextual effects, not only will they have no assurance that they have understood the text, but they are also very likely to *terminate the communication process*. That is, they will stop reading or listening.

This fact has been confirmed quite independently from relevance theory through the research carried out by Wayne Dye and reported in his book *The Bible Translation Strategy* (1980). He investigated the spiritual impact of vernacular translation in fifteen different projects in different parts of the world, trying to relate it to a number of different factors. The result was that the strongest single factor that seemed to determine the spiritual impact of these translations was what he called the "principle of personal relevance," that is, the degree to which people were able to see the relevance of the Scriptures to their own lives.

Many problems in Bible translation can be traced to a *contextual gap* between the context envisaged by the original communicator and that available to the target audience.

Now this problem is being worked on. A special working group to provide contextual information through study-notes was set up at the Triennial Workshop of the United Bible Societies in Zimbabwe. However, if I understand correctly, according to the policy of the UBS, the notes in study editions of Bibles that they publish are subject to certain constraints, one of which is that the notes can contain only information about the historical context, excluding "application" that would help the readers recognize the relevance of the biblical texts to their lives. There are no doubt very good reasons for imposing these constraints. However, from a relevance-theoretic point of view, this decision to avoid personal application does diminish the likely success of such study editions.

It is, of course, good when notes give historical information not available to the average reader, yet necessary for understanding the intended meaning of a passage. On the other hand, it should be recognized that this in itself does not guarantee that the translation will be understood: Present-day readers normally interpret the translation in the context available to them, and everything depends on whether it turns out to be optimally relevant *in this present-day context.*

Let me illustrate this with the opening chapter of Matthew's Gospel, which begins with the genealogy of Jesus. In terms of Matthew's original intentions and his original audience, this was no doubt very effective: One of his main objectives in writing this Gospel was to assure people that Jesus was the long-expected Messiah; to qualify as Messiah, the candidate would have to be of the right lineage; and it was common knowledge that the Messiah would be a descendant of King David. The identity of the Messiah was naturally a burning issue in those days of oppression by the Roman government; and so, as far as his contemporary audience was concerned, on the very first pages of his Gospel, Matthew began to tackle a crucial point.

But what about the average modern English reader? The fact that he was reading the Gospel of Matthew would indicate some interest in its contents, presumably because of Jesus, the central character of the book. Depending on the kind of religious education he may have had, he would perhaps have some biblical knowledge. Let us say he has heard of outstanding characters such as King David or Abraham. But the majority of the other individuals listed in the genealogy would very likely be unknown to him; and their names, for example, "Jehoshaphat," would be hard to read. Thus our reader would have to struggle through a long list of unfamiliar and difficult names. In terms of relevance theory, he would have to spend a lot of processing effort on the first sixteen verses of this chapter.

Despite this great processing effort, our modern reader would find little reward. He would almost certainly not be aware that Davidic lineage was important as a prerequisite for Jesus to qualify as the Messiah. Even if he were aware of this, the question whether or not Jesus is that Messiah-figure expected by the Jews would probably not be prominent in his mind. Nor is it likely that the relevance would be increased by Matthew's explicit comment after the genealogy that the lineage consisted of three sets of fourteen ancestors.

The difficulty that an English reader would have in arriving at an interpretation consistent with the principle of relevance contrasts sharply with the original communication act. First, the background knowledge available to Matthew's Jewish Christian readers would have decreased the processing effort; for example, they knew many of the names in the genealogy. Moreover, the text would have had a rich pay-off in terms of contextual implications. The strong messianic expectations of the day and the readers' familiarity with (most of) the characters in the genealogy would have enabled them to see many interesting implications in it: The mention of women in a genealogy (e.g., Rahab) and the allusion to one of the dark spots in King David's life (with the explicit statement that Solomon's mother had been someone else's wife) would have provided food for thought.

What can we conclude from this? The clear implication is that the originally intended meaning of Matthew's genealogy is not communicable to the kind of present-day English-speaking audience that we just pictured. Whether or not part of the originally intended meaning can be communicated to them depends on what kinds of contextual effects can be achieved in their present-day context.

Furthermore, simply providing the reader with additional historical information will probably not be enough to solve this problem. Materials need to be prepared that will help the receptor audience derive sufficient contextual effects in the cognitive environment they live in so that they can relate the text to their own lives.

In Western countries, where many readers have a wide general knowledge of the world and other cultures, a large body of Christian literature is being produced with the aim of helping present-day readers see the relevance of the Bible for their lives. In contrast, in Third World countries where the knowledge background of many readers is much more restricted, we usually take the line that essentially all that people need is a good translation of the biblical text. This strange state of affairs seems to have arisen from an inadequate understanding of the natural constraints to which communication is subject. This, in turn, leads to quite unrealistic expectations as to what a translation can achieve.

While we are right in having the highest regard for the Scriptures and their life-changing power, I do not find any evidence in the Bible itself that when God communicates with us, he sets aside the laws of communication that he himself has built into us. In fact, in Acts 8 we are explicitly told that the Spirit prompted Philip to approach the Ethiopian eunuch—to do what? To help the eunuch overcome the contextual gap that kept him from understanding the Scriptures! The eunuch's complaint to Philip was that he could not understand the biblical text unless someone explained it to him.

I believe that this question is still being asked today. How can they understand? The answer "You are getting a good translation" is ultimately not sufficient.

In fact, if I may say something rather heretical, one reason that we think our translations are doing quite well is that we base our judgment on our own secondhand experience. I have a strong suspicion that, even with a good background in biblical studies, for many biblical passages we are a long way from the communicative impact of the original, a long way from the rich and exciting interpretation it yielded to its readers. The reason for our misjudgment, of course, is that we have no means of processing it in the original context.

Related to this let me add a spiritual, and perhaps somewhat personal, application. Sometimes we experience what we call a "dryness" when reading the Scriptures: we do not seem to be getting anything out of them, and it may make us worried about our spiritual vitality and health. That could, of course, be the problem—I do not want to rule that out for a minute. However, there may be an alternative explanation for this experience, that is, that we are simply experiencing the natural consequences of a contextual gap. The text seems "dry" because the context in which we process it yields few contextual effects.

2.5 Further insights from the principle of relevance

Relevance theory offers a number of explanations for other phenomena that we should comment on at this point. First, it offers an explanation of *how implicit information is recovered*: It is the search for optimal relevance that leads to the recognition of implicit information. For example, the utterance "I need to be at the university really early" by itself does not yield any contextual effect in the context of the question "Can we meet early tomorrow morning?"; therefore the presumption of optimal relevance prompts the audience to look for some other piece of highly accessible contextual information that will lead to contextual effects. Such information was, in fact, readily available to me (see the second situation in sec. 1.1). Hence, relevance theory offers a plausible explanation for how the existence of implicit information is noticed and how it is recovered. (The code model, on the other hand, while it acknowledges the existence of implicit information, does not explain how it is recovered.)

Second, relevance theory explains *why there is such a thing as implicit information*: To convey information implicitly rather than explicitly is a very economical way of communication. In our example, the use of the single utterance "I need to be at the university really early" served to communicate not only the answer requested, but also the reason why a meeting would not be possible at that time. Hence, the use of implicit information is well motivated within a cost-sensitive model of human communication. (By contrast, it is hard to see within the code-model view why people would ever want to express anything other than what they meant.)

Third, the principle of relevance offers an explanation of *our intuition that utterances need to "make sense"*: "Making sense" means that they need to yield contextual effects; that is, they need to inferentially link up with the context. (The code model has no theoretical tools for handling this notion of "making sense.")

Fourth, the theory highlights and explains *why contextual information is not incidental, but crucial for the interpretation of utterances*: Utterance interpretation is motivated by the search for contextual effects, and contextual effects are obviously dependent on a context.

3
THE NOTION OF FAITHFULNESS

3.1 Recapitulation

Communication works by inference. The communicator produces a stimulus from which the addressee can infer the communicator's informative intention. This process succeeds as well as it does because of a universal psychological principle—the principle of relevance. The addressee can assume that the first interpretation consistent with this principle is the one intended by the communicator.

One of the entailments of this principle is that, in order to be communicable, the informative intention must yield adequate contextual effects for the addressees. This, in turn, means that whether or not an informative intention can be communicated to an audience depends on the contextual knowledge available to them. In view of these facts, the assumption often made in translation circles that any message can be communicated to any audience regardless of their background knowledge seems untenable.

3.2 Fidelity and equivalence

One of the central problems of translation theory (and practice, for that matter) has been that of clarifying or defining what the relationship between a source text and its translation should be. It has occupied many minds for centuries. For a long time theoreticians operated with notions like "fidelity" or "faithfulness," without, however, being able to give theoretical account of these concepts.

Attempts at defining "fidelity" as an identity relation were doomed to failure because the notion of identity turns out to be too strong—strict identity is rarely possible in translation. (From this recognition that translation cannot generally achieve identity, some have concluded that translation is impossible.) So a notion weaker than identity was needed. Thus, the notion of "equivalence" was introduced, and has found wide acceptance.

Unfortunately, the notion of "equivalence" has not so far fared much better than "fidelity." It has not been possible to find a generally acceptable definition of translation equivalence. As Svejcer (1981:321) says, "Equivalence is one of the central issues in the theory of translation and yet one on which linguists seem to have agreed to disagree."

Furthermore, serious doubts have been expressed that this concept can be tackled on a general translation theoretical basis at all. Wilss (1982:135) comes to the conclusion that

> TE [translation equivalence] cannot possibly be integrated in a general translation theory but must be looked upon as part of specific translation theories which are at best text-type-related or, even more restrictedly, single-text-oriented.

It is surprising that Wilss does not discuss the further implications of such a view for the whole enterprise of constructing a theory of translation. One of the main points of theory construction is that it should allow us to account for complex phenomena in terms of simpler ones; that is, one of its main motivations is to make generalizations about phenomena. But if it turns out that each individual phenomenon—which here is not only each text, but potentially each instance of translating it for a particular audience—may require its own theory of equivalence, then this means that these phenomena cannot be accounted for in terms of generalizations at all and that they actually fall outside the scope of theory. Thus, recognition of the potential need for single-text-based "theories" of translation equivalence entails a possible reductio ad absurdum of the notion of "theory" itself.

So it seems that the notion of "equivalence" has not led us out of the problem of defining the relationship between source text and translation, at least not up to this point. The reasons are that, first, there is no general consensus as to which of several different definitions should be adopted and, second, the definitions themselves seem to be open to different interpretations.

It is interesting that although relevance theory was not conceived with translation concerns in mind, it does offer a notion of "faithfulness." So let us examine what this is about. In order to do this, we need to start with some wider considerations. In fact, we need to take a big step back from translation first. We need to introduce two further basic notions of relevance theory: those of *interpretive resemblance* and *interpretive use*.

3.3 Interpretive resemblance

Let me begin with a quotation from Wilson and Sperber (1988a:136):

> In the appropriate circumstances, any object in the world can be used to represent any other object it resembles. A uniformed doll can be used to represent a soldier, an arrangement of cutlery and glasses can be used to represent a road accident, a set of vertical lines to represent the height

of members of a class. Such representations are used in communication for two main purposes: *to inform an audience about the properties of an original, and for the expression of attitude.*

In other words, we can exploit the resemblance one object bears to some other object to communicate something about that other object.

When do objects resemble one another? When they *share properties* with each other. Thus, the uniformed doll shares with the soldier the property of wearing a uniform; in virtue of this shared property, on occasion that doll may be used to represent a soldier. The arrangement of cutlery and glasses resembles vehicles and people involved in a road accident with regard to their movement and position relative to each other, so they can be used to represent that accident.

Like objects, utterances, too, can resemble each other. They can resemble each other in phonological properties, and we might make use of that when imitating someone's speech. More importantly to us, they can resemble one another in their meaning or inferential properties. Resemblance between utterances that is based on shared meaning properties is called *interpretive resemblance.*

For a clearer understanding of interpretive resemblance, let us consider some examples:

(a) Bill likes his new toys.
(b) William likes his new toys.

Let us assume that these two utterances refer to the same situation, and hence have the same propositional content or, as Sperber and Wilson prefer to say, the same *propositional form.* According to the inferential approach to meaning assumed in relevance theory, identity in propositional form means that the two utterances share all their implications. So, since our two utterances refer to the same situation, they share, for example, all of the following implications (note that this list is not complete):

(a) Bill likes something.
(b) Bill has new toys.
(c) Bill likes something new.
(d) Someone likes his new toys.

Whatever implications one of these two utterances has, the other also has.

As one would expect, interpretive resemblance between utterances does not have to be complete: that is, they need not share *all* their implications. Consider the following pair of utterances:

(a) Jack bought a new Mercedes.
(b) Don bought a car.

The two preceding utterances share, for example, the implication that someone bought a car. However, there are also implications that they do not share. The implication of the first utterance that Jack bought something is not an implication of the second utterance. So the interpretive resemblance between the two utterances is incomplete. Generally speaking, then, interpretive resemblance between utterances is a *matter of degree.*

As may have been noticed, in the examples considered so far we looked only at their semantic, or analytic, implications. However, interpretive resemblance is not dependent on the sharing of semantic implications, but obtains also where two utterances share contextual implications, in a certain context. Thus the utterance "For my colleague only the best is good enough" can be said to interpretively resemble the utterance in "Jack bought a new Mercedes" if the context is as follows:

(a) Someone who buys a Mercedes has money to spare.
(b) Someone for whom only the best is good enough has money to spare.
(c) Jack is my colleague.

Even though the two utterances do not share analytic implications—given the set of contextual assumptions in (a), (b), and (c)—both will yield the same contextual implication:

Jack has money to spare.

This point will be important later in our discussion.

3.4 Interpretive use

Instances where an utterance is used to represent another utterance in virtue of their interpretive resemblance are referred to as *interpretive use.* This differs from the descriptive use of utterance, where the utterances are employed in virtue of the fact that they describe some state of affairs. This distinction is a rather fundamental one, because in interpretive use the utterance is primarily intended to represent another utterance and it does not necessarily say anything about the truth or falsehood of the content of the utterance.

For example, consider the utterance "Thoughts have logical properties." If this is interpreted as an instance of descriptive use, the fact that the speaker uttered this statement would be taken to mean that she holds the assumption expressed to be true. Otherwise, she would be liable to the charge of lying.

However, someone reviewing relevance theory during a lecture might use this same statement interpretively to represent a claim made by Sperber and Wilson. In this case there is no expectation that the use of this utterance should commit the speaker to the truth of this statement. In fact, the speaker herself may reject the truth of this utterance, yet would not be liable to the charge of lying. On the other hand, if Sperber and Wilson did not hold the belief that "Thoughts have logical properties," the speaker would be liable to the charge of misrepresenting the original utterance.

It is easy to see that this distinction between the descriptive and interpretive use of utterances can be of great importance. It can give rise to serious miscommunication, especially since it need not be marked linguistically in any overt way. Consider the following example:

(a) Sarah: I really have a rather poor appetite these days.
(b) Joe: It's the Chernobyl accident.
(c) Sarah: Do you really think so?
(d) Joe: Actually, no; but Chernobyl gets blamed for anything these days, doesn't it?

In this example, (b) is obviously meant interpretively, reflecting what people, in general, believe. It is not Joe's own conviction, but there is nothing in the utterance to mark this. In fact, these two distinct modes of using utterances create a basic ambiguity which needs to be resolved for every utterance. As we shall see later on, this distinction between the interpretive use and the descriptive use of utterances does have important consequences for translation.

3.5 The notion of faithfulness

Having introduced these two notions of *interpretive resemblance* and *interpretive use*, we are now ready to deal with the notion of *faithfulness* provided by relevance theory.

The most common occurrence of interpretive use is, no doubt, when someone reports what someone else said. But, of course, whenever we are asked to give such a report, a whole range of options is open to us. Suppose I had just attended a session at a linguistic conference where Ken Pike spoke. After the session someone who had missed the lecture might come up to me and ask, "What did Pike say?" At this point, I have a wide range of options open to me:

(a) I could summarize the lecture in a couple of sentences.
(b) I could give brief summaries of each of the main points of the lecture.
(c) I might just say, "Oh, it was all about discourse."
(d) I might pick out some particular topics of Pike's talk, perhaps "cohesion," and represent in some detail what he said about that, possibly adding some explanations as well.
(e) I might offer to let him read the full written version of the paper that was handed out.

What would determine which answer I choose? According to relevance theory, my answer would, as always, be determined by considerations of relevance and, specifically, by my assumptions about what my communication partner might find optimally relevant. Suppose I know that my colleague is not interested in discourse analysis. In that case, I might choose to reply with (c). On the other hand, if I judge that my colleague is interested in cohesion, though he might not know too much about it, I would reply along the lines of (d). Or if I thought my colleague was very interested in almost anything that Pike said in his presentation, I would perhaps choose option (e).

Thus the search for optimal relevance would constrain me to express myself so that, with minimal processing effort, my colleague can derive information that is adequately relevant to him. And since his question was about what someone else said (that is, since I was engaged in interpretive use), the information conveyed by my answer would be expected to resemble what Pike was talking about rather than, for example, what Longacre said or what I thought.

Put more generally, in interpretive use the principle of relevance does, in effect, come across as a *presumption of faithfulness*. As Wilson and Sperber have put it, in interpretive use "the speaker guarantees that her utterance is a faithful enough representation of the original: that is, resembles it closely enough in relevant respects" (1988a:137). When engaging in interpretive use, what the reporter intends to convey is presumed to interpretively resemble the original (otherwise this would not be an instance of interpretive use) and it is also presumed to have adequate contextual effects without requiring gratuitous processing effort. In other words, the resemblance it shows is to be consistent with the presumption of optimal relevance.

Since this notion of faithfulness is based on the concept of relevance, it is fully *context-sensitive*. It can explain, for example, why people do not always give a verbatim report when asked what someone said: Consistency with the principle of relevance constrains them to report only those aspects of the original text or utterance that will be adequately relevant in the context available to the audience.

Now, this is not to say that the communicator will always succeed in this. An anecdote is told about Calvin Coolidge, the president of the United States known as "Silent Cal." One Sunday he came home from church, and his wife asked him what the sermon was about. He answered, "Sin."

"Well, what did the preacher say about it?" she pressed.

"He was against it."

It seems that Coolidge's wife was not satisfied that what she was told about the sermon resembled the original sermon closely enough in relevant respects. (Interestingly, this might well be taken as an instance of resemblance by sharing of contextual implications, for it is quite possible that there was no statement in the whole sermon semantically resembling the statement "The speaker is against sin.")

3.6 Faithfulness across language barriers

So far, we have looked only at the interpretive use of utterances where both the original and the report are in the same language. We might call this *intralingual interpretive use*. However, it is evident that an utterance in one language can be used to interpretively represent an utterance made in another language. To the degree that these two utterances share implications, one can be used to represent the other. In other words, there is the possibility of *interlingual interpretive use* of utterances.

How would utterances in interlingual interpretive use be interpreted? According to the same principles as interpretively used utterances within the same language. The principle of relevance would lead to an expectation of faithfulness, dependent on contextual factors.

For the most part, interlingual interpretive use offers the same range, or continuum of options, available intralingually. Going back to Pike's lecture, let us assume that the person who asked me what Pike's lecture was about understood only German. In that situation, I would have available all the options mentioned in the original version of the example: summary in a couple of sentences, summary of main points, a more detailed account of selected points, and so forth. The particular option chosen will be determined by the requirement of faithfulness which, in turn, depends on the contextual knowledge available to the target audience.

In one way, it seems that this is, in fact, all we need to say about translation; for we have explained how a text of one language can be interpretively represented by a text in another language, and we have explained how it will be interpreted. Translation seems to fall under this category of interpretive representation. Translations are representations of texts in other languages and, in order to communicate successfully, these texts must be faithful representations of the originals. That is, they must resemble the originals closely enough in respects relevant to the target audience.

We may well ask ourselves, however, whether this general notion of faithfulness is not perhaps too vague to be useful for translation. After all, "close enough resemblance in relevant respects" does not seem to determine anything very concrete.

The answer is that the principle of relevance heavily constrains the translation with regard to both what it is intended to convey and how it is expressed. Thus, if we ask in what respects the intended interpretation of the translation should resemble the original, the answer is: in respects that make it adequately relevant to the audience—that is, that offer adequate contextual effects. If we ask how the translation should be expressed, the answer is: in such a manner that it yields the intended interpretation without causing the audience unnecessary processing effort. Hence, considerations of relevance constrain the intended interpretation of the translation and also the way it is expressed; and since consistency with the principle of relevance is always context-dependent, these constraints are contextually determined.

These conditions seem to provide exactly the guidance that translators and translation theorists have been looking for. They determine *in what respects* the translation should resemble the original: only in those respects that can be expected to make it adequately relevant to the receptor-language audience. They determine also that the translation should be clear and natural in the sense that it should not be unnecessarily difficult to understand.

Let us illustrate the adequacy of this definition of faithfulness by applying it to an example. The example I want to use is given by Jiří Levý (1969). It involves a German poem by Morgenstern, "The Aesthetic Weasel":

Ein Wiesel
sass auf einem Kiesel
inmitten Bachgeriesel

Das raffinier—
te Tier
Tat's um des Reimes Willen.

[A weasel
sat on a pebble
in the midst of a ripple of a brook.

The shrewd
animal
did it for the sake of the rhyme. (Translation my own)]

Levy discusses Max Knight's English translation of the first part of
this little poem:

A weasel
perched on an easel
within a patch of teasel

He then presents four alternatives, two of which we look at here:

A ferret
nibbling a carrot
in a garret

A mink
sipping a drink
in a kitchen sink

In evaluating these three renderings, Levy claims that all three
are equally possible translations; for, he says, "More important than
the individual meanings in detail is here the preservation of the play
on words" (p. 103).

How does this matter look in our relevance-theoretic approach?

Starting from Levy's last observation, we can account for this
intuition if we assume that the relevance of the original depended
not so much on the assumption it conveyed about the activity of a
certain weasel, namely, that he sat on a pebble in a stream, but
rather in the suggestion that the animal acted in this way with a
literary motive in mind, to give rise to a rhyming poem.

It is this amusing assumption that seems to be primarily
responsible for the relevance of the original. Hence, Levy's intuition

that this assumption is particularly important can be accounted for in terms of relevance.

However, it does not follow that preservation of those more important "abstract" features necessarily frees the translator from the obligation to preserve any of the more "concrete" semantic properties of the first half of the poem, as Levy seems to suggest by treating the other renderings as equally possible translations. It is not difficult to see that these last two alternatives differ from the original in certain assumptions that they could reasonably be expected to share. (Knight's translation shows them.) Thus, there is a sense in which the alternative renderings differ from the original in unnecessary and rather arbitrary respects.

This intuition can be explained in terms of our relevance-based definition of faithfulness, faithfulness having to do with the resemblance of a translation to the original in relevant respects. The two alternatives lack, for example, resemblance in that Morgenstern's poem was about a weasel, not a ferret, lizard, or some other animal. (In relevance-theoretic terms, the analytic implication "A weasel did something" is not shared.) The fact that it was a *weasel* may well be relevant (e.g., for someone interested in the imagery Morgenstern uses in his poems). If so, then the alternate versions are less faithful than they could reasonably have been; they fail to resemble the original adequately in this relevant respect, given that this resemblance could have been retained without increasing the processing effort, as Knight's translation shows.

This last point is important. Sometimes it is possible to achieve a higher degree of resemblance but only at the cost of increasing the processing effort that is not outweighed by gains in contextual effects. Since this would result in a loss of overall relevance, the rendering showing less resemblance will usually be the one required for successful communication.

Thus, we see here that the notion of faithfulness helps us to spell out and explain quite concretely our intuitions about some of the shortcomings of these alternative renderings. It is not vague at all when applied to a particular text, but is capable of quite concrete and context-specific predictions.

At the same time, the example also illustrates the need for this context-sensitive notion of faithfulness. Consider again my own auxiliary translation, or gloss, provided earlier:

A weasel
sat on a pebble
in the midst of a ripple of a brook.

The shrewd
animal
did it for the sake of the rhyme.

This rendering obviously does *not* attempt to preserve the rhyme; hence, it would not serve well to convey the main assumption mentioned above. It would leave the English reader somewhat puzzled. At the same time, this gloss did not seem irrelevant or inappropriate to our discussion at the point where it was presented. Again, this follows from our definition of faithfulness which calls for resemblance in *relevant* respects. It *is* relevant because some readers may not know enough German to understand the semantic content of the poem. This translation helps them by giving them easy access to its semantically determined meaning, and knowledge of that meaning is relevant to the overall thrust of our discussion.

Thus, it would seem that the relevance theory of faithfulness is indeed useful: It allows very concrete judgment and yet is flexible enough to adapt to different contextual requirements.

However, we may wonder whether or not it is possible to define some fixed notion of translation that would be context independent, so that one would get what could, in some sense, be defined as the same message, whether the receptors were Zulus or Eskimos. Relevance theory does offer this possibility, and we shall consider this question in the fifth lecture.

4
NONLITERAL LANGUAGE

4.1 Recapitulation

In the previous lecture we saw that different utterances can have the same implications. Just as one object can be used to represent another for communicative purposes, so utterances, too, can be used to represent other utterances which they resemble. This use of utterances is called *interpretive use.* In interpretive use the principle of relevance raises an expectation of faithfulness, that is, that the representing utterance resemble the original closely enough in relevant respects. We saw that this notion of faithfulness can be applied to intralingual as well as interlingual interpretive use. We saw, furthermore, that this notion has the flexibility to cover a wide spectrum of different cases of interpretive use and yet allows context-specific evaluations at the same time.

In this lecture we want to look at further applications of interpretive use, which will allow us to deal with some of the more sublime rhetorical possibilities of language.

4.2 Interpretive resemblance between thought and utterance

In the previous lecture we said that utterances can interpretively resemble each other by virtue of the fact that they have implications in common. But it is not only utterances that have implications; thoughts have implications, too. Therefore there can be a relation of interpretive resemblance between thoughts and utterances.

Furthermore, just as there can be varying degrees of resemblance between utterances, so utterances can resemble to varying degrees the thoughts they are intended to express. An utterance that shares all its implications with the thought it expresses is called a *literal* interpretation of that thought. To say that an utterance is less than strictly literal is to say that it shares *some*, but not all, of its implications with the thought it is meant to convey.

Going back to our earlier example, let us assume that "William likes his new toys" is a thought, rather than an utterance. (We shall show this in the text by using capital letters.)

(a) Thought: WILLIAM LIKES HIS NEW TOYS.
(b) Utterance: Bill likes his new toys.

In this case, the utterance expresses a literal interpretation of the thought, sharing all its implications. However, utterances do not have to be literal interpretations of the thoughts they represent.

One evening, as I sat in my room typing away at the computer, Ronald Sim, who shared the room with me, suddenly said, "It's seven o'clock." He intended me to derive the contextual implication that we should go for supper. When I looked at my watch, it was actually 6:57 P.M., plus a few seconds, which Ronald confirmed when I asked him. Had Ronald lied to me, giving me the wrong time? Of course not. In fact, I would probably have found it rather funny if he had said: "It is now 6:57 P.M., and 24 seconds."

It does not take much investigation to see that we engage in this kind of "loose talk" all the time, to use an expression of Sperber and Wilson. We say "It's steaming hot in here," even if there is no sign of steam at all. In literature, writers refer to Ethiopia as "the roof of Africa," even though it does not cover anything, and so forth.

It has sometimes been claimed in literary studies (also, incidentally, in Grice's approach) that these usages are, in some way, abnormal, as though the norm is to speak the literal truth, and "loose talk" breaks or violates this norm. But, in fact, we break the so-called norm as much as we keep it.

Within relevance theory there is no reason to assume that literal utterances are somehow "more normal" than freer ways of expression. Let me quote from Sperber and Wilson (1986a:233):

> The speaker is presumed to aim at optimal relevance, not at literal truth. The optimal interpretive expression of a thought should give the hearer information about that thought which is relevant enough to be worth processing, and should require as little processing effort as possible. There are many quite ordinary situations where a literal utterance is not optimally relevant: for example where the effort needed to process it is not offset by the gain in information conveyed.

That explains why Ronald said to me, "It's seven o'clock," rather than "It's now 6:57 P.M. and 24 seconds." The second utterance would have required more processing effort on my part, without yielding any additional contextual effects beyond the fact that it was time to go for supper—except, perhaps, that Ronald must be an extremely pedantic person, which is not what he intended to communicate!

In another context, however, matters may be different. Thus a newscaster who is scheduled to read the seven o'clock news may well be told that the time is already 6:57 and some seconds.

In general, the relation between an utterance and the thought it expresses is one of faithfulness: the utterance is expected to resemble the thought or thoughts it represents closely enough in relevant respects. Thus, in relevance theory, the use of less than literal expressions does not involve the violation of any norm; it is a perfectly normal way of communication. (The idea that literalism constitutes a norm of some sort goes back to the code model of communication.)

4.3 Metaphors

The nonliteral uses of language (e.g., metaphor) find a very natural explanation in relevance theory. Suppose I had a somewhat complex thought I wanted to communicate. For example, I might want to communicate that an acquaintance of mine by the name of Bill tends to be rather threatening in his business behavior and to bully people, that he does so with the help of other equally sinister people, and that he tends to be ruthless in his practices. I could, of course, express all these thoughts separately by more or less literal expressions:

(a) Bill tends to be rather threatening in his business practices.
(b) He bullies people.
(c) He is ruthless.
(d) There are also these sinister-looking guys he hangs around with.

But suppose I found a *single*, simple utterance that would communicate *all* of these thoughts equally well; considerations of relevance would lead me to use that single expression. The only complication is that the expression I have in mind has some implications that I definitely do not intend to communicate. I could still use that expression as the most economical stimulus—*provided my audience has some way of distinguishing the implications that I want to communicate from those that I do not.* If this condition were fulfilled, then I could still go ahead and use that simple utterance.

As we have already seen, the audience does not, in any case, automatically expect the utterance I express to *completely* resemble the thought I intend to convey. Rather, the audience will expect to discover, by consistency with the principle of relevance, what the intended resemblances are. This same expectation applies to the case just considered. Since the principle of relevance thus offers a means for differentiating intended and unintended meaning, I may well be able to use that simple utterance without necessarily endorsing its full and literal meaning. For the previous example about Bill, the following utterance would serve well:

Bill is a gangster.

Under appropriate contextual conditions, this expression could indeed communicate the four thoughts previously listed without, however, conveying the full literal meaning of the expression, which might, for example, entail that Bill has a criminal record. (Many other nonliteral usages of language like hyperbole and metonomy can be accounted for along similar lines.)

Does this mean that the metaphorical "Bill is a gangster" communicates the same meaning as the sequence of utterances that listed four various ideas? The answer is no. There is a very significant difference between these two instances of communication with regard to the *relative strength* with which the thoughts are communicated in each case.

4.4 Degrees of strength of communication

The other day Wren Ross shared with me the following conversational exchange he had with his three-year-old son:

(a) Father: Do you want Chinese rice?
(b) Son: I don't like vegetables.

In this example, Ron's son did not give a direct answer to his father. Rather, he expected him to infer it from his reply. The answer expressed by itself does not yield any contextual effects with his father's question, which forms the initial context, so his father had to expand this context, looking for one or more further contextual assumptions that would lead to contextual effects when combined with the utterance. In this case there was one very definite assumption of their shared cognitive environment which the son intended his father to use:

There are vegetables in Chinese rice.

Once we add this assumption to the context, we obtain the contextual implication that the son does not want any rice.

By expressing himself in this indirect way, the son very clearly prompted his father to supply some assumption not only *like* the one we quoted, but (at least) *exactly* this assumption. Without it, the answer could not be seen to be consistent with the principle of relevance. The fact that this particular assumption, "There are vegetables in Chinese rice," is crucial for establishing the relevance of this utterance makes it a *strongly communicated assumption*, in this case, a *strong implicature*. One of the characteristics of strong implicatures is that the communicator takes the responsibility for their truth.

Not all implicatures, however, are strong. Suppose Stephen is just getting acquainted with a nice girl named Melanie. He'd like to go out with her, but has no idea what sort of things she likes. He'd like to suggest that they see *Jaws 17* which has just come to the local movie theater. However, he'd hate to be turned down with his first suggestion. So he might just say:

> I hear there's a new movie in town, *Jaws 17*.

Now, by presenting this utterance to Melanie, Stephen communicates the presumption of optimal relevance, that is, his belief that this utterance will have adequate contextual effects for her. However, he is giving her no indication as to any particular contextual effects he expects her to derive. So Melanie might take Stephen's remark simply as an indication that he wants to make conversation and that he is suggesting a topic that may be worth talking about. On the other hand, if Melanie had actually been thinking about going to this movie, she could take Stephen's remark to indicate that he has some interest in this movie. Of course, Melanie could also draw the implication that Stephen wants to find out what she thinks about the film, and she might even suspect that he is considering inviting her to this movie.

However, since Stephen has given her no evidence for believing that he actually intends her to draw any one of these inferences in particular, none of these implications is strongly communicated. Regardless of which of these interpretations Melanie might choose, she would significantly share in the responsibility for the validity of her interpretation. Thus, while the intention to invite her to the movie was within the range of possible interpretations, Stephen had given her no evidence to believe that this was the case. So, if she responded, "Oh, thanks for the invitation, Stephen!" he would probably be rather surprised.

Thus, in contrast to our earlier example of father and son, here Stephen (the communicator) gives no evidence by the way he talks that he has in mind any particular contextual effect he expects his hearer to obtain. The only presumption made is that the hearer is in a position to derive adequate contextual effects, whatever they might be. This entitles the hearer to use any of the assumptions that come to mind and that the communicator could have expected. However, it also means that none of the implicatures derived in this way is strongly supported by the communicator: rather, there is a *range of comparatively weak implicatures.*

Sperber and Wilson (1986a:199) characterize the relative strength of implicatures as follows:

> Strong implicatures are those premises and conclusions . . . which the hearer is strongly encouraged but not actually forced to supply. The weaker the encouragement, and the wider the range of possibilities among which the hearer can choose, the weaker the implicatures. Eventually . . . a point is reached at which the hearer receives no encouragement at all to supply any particular premise and conclusion, and he takes the entire responsibility for supplying them himself.

This recognition helps us to see that there is a very significant difference between using the metaphor "Bill is a gangster" and expressing each of the thoughts explicitly: Expressing each thought explicitly would mean that each thought was strongly communicated. I, the communicator, would be held fully responsible for the truth of each of these affirmations. Not so with the use of the metaphor. I could not, for example, be nailed down as having asserted, in particular, that Bill was ruthless, because I had not given any evidence that I intended to communicate this particular thought.

It is often claimed that a metaphor is a formal device that serves to embellish a text. We are also told that it usually has one basic point of similarity that constitutes the meaning of the metaphor and that can be expressed in nonfigurative language. On the basis of this claim we, as translators, are encouraged to replace a metaphor by plain-language expressions if the metaphor is not readily understood.

In fact, as we have seen just now, metaphors are not formal devices with an embellishing function; rather, they are needed to get the communicator's intended meaning across. In fact, they may be the only way in which she can fulfil her intention of communicating additional weaker implications. Furthermore, the view that metaphors have usually one "point of similarity," or "ground of comparison," is as erroneous as the claim that its meaning can be conveyed equally well by an expression in plain language. The implicit claim of relevance theory is that this is never the case—otherwise consistency with the principle of relevance would have required the speaker to use the plain-language expression. As Sperber and Wilson put it, "the speaker must have intended to convey something more than this if the relative indirectness of the utterance is to be justified" (1986a:236).

4.5 Poetic effects

This possibility of weak communication is responsible for the immense richness of language referred to by Sperber and Wilson (1986a) as "poetic effects." To allay the fears of those who are worried that relevance theory might not be applicable to literature, let us look at a passage in John's Gospel. I am thinking of the passage where John reports how Judas left from the Last Supper to betray Jesus. The passage ends with the words "As soon as Judas had taken the bread he went out. And it was night" (John 13:30, NIV).

Let me suggest that the little comment "And it was night," in the Greek only three short words, ἦν δὲ νύξ, communicates much more than the time of day. It is a very rich final chord at the end of this dramatic section.

The door of the house opens, throwing a bright square of light across the pavement. Judas's shadow appears, leaving only a small edge of light around his dark figure. As Judas walks into the night, his head, his shoulders vanish, finally the whole man is swallowed up by the darkness. Judas left the brightness of Jesus and his company behind him, left the light and preferred the darkness: "This is the verdict: Light has come into the world, but men loved darkness instead of light because their deeds were evil" (John 3:19).

Ἦν δὲ νύξ—it was night not only *around* Judas, but also in his heart. He was utterly disappointed with this Jesus, there was no use following him. He had given up on him—night had settled on Judas's mind, urging him to carry out his sinister plan.

Ἦν δὲ νύξ—it is dangerous to walk in the night, Judas. "The man who walks in the dark does not know where he is going" (John 12:35). Stepping out into the night, Judas was going to his own destruction, but he did not know it.

Ἦν δὲ νύξ—with Judas's departure, night had also fallen on the work of Jesus, as he had expected: "Night is coming when no one can work" (John 9:4). He had said, "You are going to have the light just a little while longer" (John 12:35). Now the night had come —ἦν δὲ νύξ.

Three little words, an immensely rich interpretation. How does it come about? By including these words, John promised his readers adequate contextual effects. However, he refrained from giving them particular guidance as to what these effects might be, inviting them to explore and exploit the richness of the cognitive environment he shared with them.

While it seems presumptuous to attempt a full reconstruction of that cognitive environment, we can at least sketch a few parts of it.

Night (encyclopedic information)
- people sleep at night
- schema of someone leaving a house at night
- things Jesus said about the night: "Night is coming when no one can work"
- evil people often carry out their sinister schemes at night
- it is dark at night

Dark (encyclopedic information)
- one cannot see or be seen in the dark
- walking in the dark is dangerous
- one can't see where one is going in the dark
- people's hearts can be said to be dark
- people are scared of the dark
- things Jesus said about the dark: "The man who walks in the dark does not know where he is going."

We could discuss how these various pieces of information would be accessed and scanned for implicatures. Note that the same information may be stored in different ways in memory. For example, the fact that one cannot see where one is going in the dark may be stored in the memory, both as common knowledge and as a saying of Jesus. If accessed as a saying of Jesus, it may well make accessible further information about the occasion when Jesus said it, which may lead to further contextual effects, and so forth.

Sperber and Wilson (1986a:236–37) sum up how poetic effects arise:

> In general, the wider the range of potential implicatures and the greater the hearer's responsibility for constructing them, the more poetic the effect, the more creative the metaphor . . . In the richest and most successful cases, the hearer or reader can go beyond just exploring the immediate context and the entries for concepts involved in it, accessing a wide area of knowledge . . . and getting more and more very weak implicatures, with suggestions for further processing. The result is a quite complex picture, for which the hearer has to take a large part of responsibility, but the discovery of which has been triggered by the writer. The surprise or beauty of a successful creative metaphor lies in this condensation, in the fact that a single expression . . . will determine a very wide range of acceptable weak implicatures.

I think I spent more than half an hour pondering those three words, and did not exhaust their interpretation but kept on discovering new, exciting insights, in other words, contextual effects. "Oh, the depth of the riches of the wisdom and knowledge of God!" (Rom. 11:33).

Have we ever praised God enough for giving us this most marvelous faculty to communicate with each other in such rich ways? Aren't you glad God decided not to make us communicate by something as boring as the encoding and decoding of messages? I am.

4.6 Irony

Now let us turn to irony, a rather different kind of nonliteral use of language. This is a topic that Wilson and Sperber discuss at length in their article "On Verbal Irony" (1989), and I am drawing heavily on that article in this section. Wilson and Sperber begin their discussion with the following example:

> Some years ago, a referendum was held on whether Britain should enter the Common Market. There was a long campaign beforehand: television programs were devoted to it; news magazines brought out special issues. At the height of the campaign, an issue of the satirical magazine *Private Eye* appeared. On the cover was a photograph of spectators at a village cricket match, sprawled in deck chairs, heads lolling, fast asleep and snoring; underneath was the caption: "The Common Market—The Great Debate." (p. 96)

An obvious piece of verbal irony. But what is irony? In classical rhetoric, verbal irony is a trope, a nonliteral use of language. Definitions usually assert that the figurative meaning of the ironic expression is the opposite of its literal meaning: Irony is the opposite of what is said. Modern pragmatic analyses follow the same lines; thus according to Grice, "the ironist deliberately flouts the maxim of truthfulness, implicating the opposite of what was literally said" (Wilson and Sperber 1989:97).

However, these definitions are inadequate because there are a number of instances that we would intuitively call ironic but that do not fall under these definitions. One of these is *ironical understatement*, an instance of which is the following passage from *Romeo and Juliet*, where Mercutio makes an ironical comment on his death-wound (quoted in Wilson and Sperber 1989:97): "No, 'tis not so deep as a well, nor so wide as a church door, but 'tis enough, 'twill serve." This type of irony is not covered by the previous definitions: Mercutio's remark is not intended to communicate that his wound is not deep or wide enough, nor that it would not serve.

Likewise, ironical quotations do not fit the classical definition. For example, suppose someone says on a cold, windy day in spring in England: "Oh to be in England now that April's there," a quotation from Browning's "Home Thoughts from Abroad." Wilson and Sperber point out that "to succeed as irony, [this remark] must be recognized as a quotation, and not treated merely as communicating the opposite of what is literally said" (1989:98).

Furthermore, there are many cases where saying the opposite of what one means has no ironic effect at all. In their book, Sperber and Wilson (1986a:240) give the following illustration:

> Suppose we are out for a drive and you stop to look both ways before joining the main road. The road is clear, but as you are about to drive on I say quietly,
>
> (113) There's something coming.
>
> You slam on your brakes and look both ways, but the road is as clear as before. When you ask me what on earth I was doing, I explain gently that I was merely trying to reassure you that the road was clear. My utterance satisfies the classical definition of irony. I have said something which is patently false, and there is a logically related assumption, namely (114), which I could truthfully have expressed:
>
> (114) There's nothing coming.
>
> Why do you not instantly leap to the conclusion that this is what I was trying to convey?

So the classical definition breaks down in both directions: ironical statements do not always mean the opposite from what is said, and meaning the opposite of what one says does not necessarily result in irony.

How, then, can we account for irony?

When we introduced the fact that any object can be used to represent another object which it resembles, we said that this practice can serve two purposes: ". . . to inform an audience about the properties of an original, and for the expression of attitude" (Sperber and Wilson 1986a:136).

When talking about interpretive use, we discussed only the first purpose: that an interpretively used utterance can serve to give information about the content of the original utterance. Now as we try to explain irony, we come to the second purpose: that one can use an utterance interpretively to communicate an attitude to what someone said or thinks. This kind of interpretive use, in which the main thing one wants to get across is an attitude to some thought or utterance, is called *echoic* use.

Put in relevance theory terms, we can explain the difference between the two kinds of interpretive use as follows. The ordinary interpretive use achieves relevance by the information it provides about the original; echoic interpretive use achieves relevance by "informing the hearer of the fact that the speaker has in mind what so-and-so-said, and has a certain attitude to it" (Sperber and Wilson 1986a:238).

Let's see how this works by applying it to the magazine cover about the "Great Debate."

There are two main elements: the picture of the village cricket match and the caption "The Common Market—The Great Debate." The caption by itself might simply be intended to inform the readers that this issue contained a report on the debate about Britain joining the Common Market. This would have been a possible interpretation were it not for the accompanying picture. If *all* the editor intended to communicate was to notify the audience that the magazine contained a report of the debate, then the picture would have been unnecessary, requiring gratuitous processing effort from the readers. Therefore, by deliberately presenting this picture with the caption, the communicator must have intended to communicate *more* than that. What could that be?

Anybody who had been reading the papers and listening to the news in those days would have immediately recognized the expression "The Great Debate" as the "in phrase" of the day. Thus he would have recognized that this phrase was being used interpretively. Furthermore, it would have brought to his mind the various things that had been said and written about the prospect of Britain joining the Common Market, especially the expectation that this issue would cause a heated public debate. It would also have been evident to him that the addition of the picture was deliberate, intended to communicate something with regard to the caption.

What could the picture be intended to communicate? It would be rather obvious to assume that it was intended to communicate what the editor thought of this debate—that it was as boring as a village match where the players had actually dozed off. To call such a boring affair "The Great Debate" would obviously be ridiculous. So by putting this particular picture with the caption, the editor intended to communicate to his readers that he disapproved of the phrase "The Great Debate" and that it had, in fact, turned out to be quite ridiculous. Hence, his informative intention was to communicate an attitude of ridicule to the phrase "The Great Debate" and to the views it represented.

Note that this analysis does not rely on the classical definition of irony (meaning the opposite of what is said). Yet it shows how this understanding can have arisen: in many cases echoic use can imply that the communicator does not believe what is said to be true. However, this is not a defining feature, but depends on the case in question.

It is well worth noting that communicators do not necessarily give clear clues about their echoic intentions. In fact, there need be no overt clues at all that would give away the communicator's intention—she may simply assume that her attitude will be clear to you from what you know about her beliefs and assumptions.

A good example of this is Mark 7:9: "And he said to them, You have a fine way of setting aside the commands of God in order to observe your own traditions." Only contextual assumptions reveal that this statement is meant ironically. (The statement at the beginning of verse 6, which is parallel in structure, is not ironic at all.)

I once heard the following extreme case of covert irony. Two scientists had been writing articles against one another's views for some time. Suddenly one of them published a paper that seemed to be saying exactly what his opponent had always said. As soon as the other scientist read that article, he wrote him a letter, expressing his joy that his colleague had finally seen the light. To his great disappointment he had to learn that there had been no change of heart at all; the whole paper was intended as a single piece of irony, making fun of his views. So recognizing the right contextual assumptions is crucial for understanding irony.

4.7 Structural rhetorical devices

Many languages have developed special structural patterns for poetic uses: meter, rhythm, rhyme, chiastic structures, and so on. How can we account for the existence of such patterns in relevance-theoretic terms?

Jiři Levy, a scholar of translation studies whose insights are especially helpful, provides us with some essential clues. He observes that basically what these devices do is loosen relationships encoded by the grammar of the language and create new relations between parts of texts that would otherwise be unrelated (Levy 1969:174):

> A weakening of syntactic relations in verse follows simply from the fact that these are not the only organizing factors. The continuity of the sentence in verse is broken by verse boundaries . . . , and conversely individual parts that do not cohere syntactically are linked by rhyme and

other formal parallelisms. All this contributes to the independence of smaller segments and a weakening of connectives and syntactic functions. (translation my own)

While these observations in themselves do not explain much, they put us on the right road to understanding the communicative value of these artificial structural constraints.

Interference with the normal grammatical patterns of the language will first of all tend to increase the processing cost for the audience. Hence, when a poet rearranges parts of a sentence into a nonstandard or even ungrammatical order to fit patterns of rhyme or rhythm, she makes it harder for her readers to process that sentence. She can do this and maintain consistency with the principle of relevance only if this increase in processing cost is outweighed by an increase in contextual effects. This means that the deliberate imposition of such poetic structures leads to the expectation of additional contextual effects. Departures from "normal" structure that fail to compensate the hearer's additional expenditure of effort by additional contextual effects are felt to be awkward, unnatural. (Thus relevance theory offers an explanation of what is behind our intuition that an expression is "unnatural": it is the fact that it requires processing effort, without any reward in terms of meaning.)

But how can the imposition of new structural orders actually achieve an increase in contextual effects?

The answer is not difficult. According to relevance theory, poetic effects typically arise when the audience is induced and given freedom to open up and explore a wide range of contextual effects, none of which are very strongly implicated, but which, taken together, create a rich impression.

Now in prose, as Levy (1969) points out, the interpretation of the utterance follows the syntactic organization of the utterance: Concepts are grouped together and interpreted in terms of their syntactic relations, and of course one important function of syntactic relations is to specify the *semantic* relations between the various constituents of the sentence. In this way syntactic structure is one of the essential properties of natural language that allow it to work with a degree of precision not normally afforded by nonverbal communication.

In poetry, however, this very precision is often undesirable: It narrows down rather than expands the range of possible interpretations.

When using poetic devices like rhyme and rhythm, the poet imposes phonological patterns that are independent of syntactic structure and may indeed crosscut it. These patterns serve to enrich the interpretation, first because they give rise to additional groupings, and second because, in contrast to syntactic relations, the relations they suggest are semantically unspecified and so again allow greater freedom in interpretation.

The following lines from Shakespeare's "Sonnet V" may serve to illustrate this:

> Then, were not summer's distillation left
> A liquid prisoner pent in walls of glass,
> Beauty's effect with beauty were bereft,
> Nor it, nor no remembrance what it was;
> But flowers distill'd, though they with winter meet,
> Leese but their show: their substance still lives sweet.

Here, the boundary at the end of the first line induces the reader to consider this verse on its own, though syntactically the end of the sentence is not reached yet and there is a corresponding effect in the second and third line. Thus the reader is invited to dwell on and look for rewarding effects not only from the sentence as a whole, but also from each part separately, as divided by the verse boundaries.

Conversely, though the fourth line is not linked to the other parts of the poem by any particular syntactic or logical function, it is presented as an integral part of it by its conformity to the formal structure. Again the audience is challenged to explore its relationship to the content of those other parts.

Chiasm works in similar ways. The chiastic structure encourages the reader to look for additional contextual effects by relating not only adjacent but also chiastically related lines to each other. Again, the artificiality of the structure suggests that there will be such additional benefits.

Does the reader need to recognize these structures for what they are? Minimally he has to recognize them as deliberate rather than incidental; otherwise he will miss the presumption of increased relevance and hence find the utterance to be inconsistent with the principle of relevance. However, the more familiar the reader is with these devices, the easier it will be for him to process them; hence the more relevant they will turn out for him. Furthermore, the recognition that the poet used these particular rhetorical devices, and how he did so, may lead to additional contextual effects, quite apart from the actual content of the poetic text.

4.8 Other stylistic effects

Relevance theory offers explanations also for metonymy, onomatopoeic uses of language, stylistic features, focus, discourse connectives, and other special phenomena of language. A number of these are treated in my book (Gutt 1991).

4.9 Implications for the translator

We have seen that relevance theory offers explanations not only for ordinary everyday conversation, but also for phenomena that have often been claimed to be beyond the reach of analysis or scientific explanation. What does this mean for the translator?

The good news is that it offers a sharp tool for getting a better understanding of the original text and also for the analysis of translation problems. The bad news is that it shows us that translation is probably even more challenging in some respects than we had previously assumed. The richness of nonliteral meaning and its strong dependence on a shared cognitive environment may bring home to us with new clarity the question, How can the translator get this meaning across to an audience of another culture?

5

TRANSLATION AND SUCCESSFUL COMMUNICATION

5.1 Recapitulation

As seen in the fourth lecture, relevance theory explains why figurative language exists and how it works. The crucial factor for successful communication, especially when figures are employed, is that both the communicator and the audience share the same cognitive environment.

Now we turn our attention to defining an *absolute* notion of translation and then to seeing what conclusions we can draw for translation work.

5.2 Defining translation in absolute terms

In the third lecture, we discussed the notion of faithfulness for interpretive use in general. We saw that, since the communicative success of interpretive use depends on it, this notion is crucial both for intralingual and interlingual instances of such communication. Hence, this notion of faithfulness is fully applicable to translation. It is wide enough to cover all and any kind of translation; it is specific enough to make concrete predictions for each particular context.

We ended the third lecture by raising the question as to whether or not it is possible to define translation in absolute terms, independently of the context of the target audience. If a text has a fixed, that is, speaker-intended meaning, should not its translation therefore be fixed, too?

5.3 Direct versus indirect speech quotations

To explore the possibility of defining such a fixed, receptor-context-independent notion of translation, let us first consider the distinction between direct and indirect speech quotations.

Recently, a church leader in an African country was quoted to me as saying that he would never advise foreigners to leave the country in an emergency situation. Knowing that this leader had actually recalled some missionaries from dangerous locations to the capital, this statement surprised me, and I began to wonder whether the leader had perhaps been misunderstood. Perhaps he had said that he would never *tell* a missionary to leave the country, that is, never impose that decision on anybody against their will. This would be different from advising them on what might be best for them personally.

Realizing that what I was given was a free rendering of his words, I asked my source the actual word used by the leader: Did he say *advise* or was it *tell?* On other occasions I probably would not have cared which word was used; but for certain reasons, in this case the distinction was highly relevant to me. Note that, in this particular instance, it was not the utterance as a whole that I was interested in but one word in it.

This example illustrates why, at times, we want a direct speech report rather than an indirect one; it is usually when we need to know what the original communicator actually *said*.

What, then, is a direct quotation? A direct quotation is essentially a *reproduction of the original stimulus.* In other words, when using a direct quotation, we produce another token of the original phrase, sentence, text, whatever it might have been. By producing another token of the original stimulus, we preserve and therefore inform the receptor audience of all the properties of the original utterance.

But why should that be of interest in communication? There can be a number of different motivations: You may want to make an investigation into how that person speaks, what vocabulary or grammatical structures she uses, and so forth.

However, the most common motivation for using a direct quotation is probably that it gives the audience the potential to get at the full, authentic meaning intended in the original. This follows from the inferential or, if you wish, causal interdependence that the principle of relevance establishes between stimuli, context, and interpretation. This is to say, if two stimuli with identical properties are processed in the same context, they will lead to the same interpretation because they inferentially interact by the same principle—the principle of relevance. Thus, if both stimuli have the same properties, and if the contexts in which they are processed are also identical, then their propositional forms and/or descriptions, their contextual effects, the processing effort required, and the evaluation of optimal relevance will all be the same, leading to identical interpretations. This claim obviously requires some *ceteris paribus* hedging; for example, mental fatigue may lead to distortion of the interpretation.

It is this fact of providing potential access to the authentic meaning of the original which makes direct quotations of special interest for communication. And not only do they make the original interpretation accessible to the audience, they do so *without reliance on anybody else's understanding or interpretation of the original.*

The school that our children attend in Addis Ababa expects the children to memorize Scripture verses and passages. As a result, our youngest, nine years old, can quote directly and accurately to me quite a number of Scripture passages, including some that pose considerable exegetical problems, whether she understands them or not. As we know, devotees of Islam and other religions can recite direct quotations even from languages that they do not understand. This is possible because direct quotation simply relies on *reproducing another token of the original utterance.* It makes certain demands on memory and reproductive skills, but it does not require an understanding of the meaning.

This last point can be of great importance. A direct quotation frees us from someone else's interpretation. It eliminates the risk that the speech reporter may have misinterpreted the original in some way and that we might follow his misinterpretation. It also eliminates the risk that the reporter may have failed in giving us a faithful interpretation not because he did not understand correctly, but because he did not succeed in communicating it aright. All that a direct quotation requires is imitative skills and a good memory—the reporter's interpretive skills don't matter.

In this respect, direct quotations differ sharply from indirect quotations. Indirect quotations simply cannot be produced without interpreting the original utterance: One cannot summarize, paraphrase, or elaborate on an original text without having derived its interpretation first.

Thus we see that direct quotations have the advantage of giving us potential access to the intended interpretation of the original. They minimize the risk of misinterpretation through an intermediate reporter.

However, having said this, we also need to be aware of a special *constraint* that applies to direct quotations. The fact that we have been given an accurate direct quotation in no way automatically guarantees that we will arrive at the originally intended interpretation. Whether we do or not depends on whether we process this direct quotation using the contextual assumptions envisaged by the original author. Even if the direct quotation we were given is accurate, we can still misinterpret the text by using wrong contextual assumptions. This is why we said it gives the receptor audience *potential* access to the authentic meaning of the original.

In other words, even when given a direct quotation, we have to beware of the dangers created by secondary communication. *The gain in authenticity that a direct quotation promises is subject to the constraint that it must be interpreted in the originally envisaged context.*

The fact that the meaning of direct quotations is context dependent is much appreciated by politicians; even when they have been directly quoted as having made a foolish remark, they can always claim that they are being quoted "out of context." And it seems that, due to the complexities of utterance interpretation, disproving such a claim is usually too much bother for journalists to undertake.

Indirect quotations, by contrast, do not have a built-in requirement of familiarity with the context. They are produced with the addressee in mind, entitling him to start from the most accessible contextual information, looking for consistency with the principle of relevance in the usual fashion.

5.4 Direct and indirect quotation across languages

What about direct and indirect quotations from one language to another? We already saw from the example about reporting Pike's lecture (see sec. 3.5) that there is no problem of principle with *indirect* quotations from one language into another. But what about interlingual *direct* quotation?

Perhaps you noticed already that I did not mention this as an option when adapting our example to interlingual interpretive use. The simple reason was, of course, that giving a monolingual speaker of German a copy of the speech in English would be rather pointless: It would not help him to cross the language barrier.

Furthermore, there is no other *mechanical* process comparable to direct quotation by which we could somehow reproduce the stimuli (words, sentences, paragraphs, whatever) of the source language by corresponding stimuli in the target language. There is no algorithm by which we can relate the Greek sentence ἦν δὲ νύξ to the English sentence "and it was night" that would promise us access to the authentic interpretation of the original *apart from the meaning of these words.*

The relations between any of the elements of these two sentences is one of *meaning:* The English sentence contains the words *it was* because their meaning resembles that of the Greek word ἦν—for no other reason. It contains the word *night* because its meaning resembles that of the Greek word νύχ—for no other reason. And it contains the word *and* because it resembles the Greek word δέ. More importantly, the whole utterance "and it was night" was composed as a translation because it interpretively resembles the Greek utterance ἦν δὲ νύξ in meaning.

Thus, whether we like it or not, across languages we *lack* the option of using a direct quotation or a similarly mechanical reproduction. (Machine translation is no exception to this. Though mechanical in some ways, it is totally dependent on the meaning relationships human beings have first established and programmed into the machine.)

Furthermore, since the meaning of a word or utterance is not in some mysterious way contained in the black ink on the paper nor in the sound waves of the utterance, but in the minds of the people using them, *translation necessarily requires the bridge of thought.* There is no other link. In this sense the call by some theorists for "meaning-based translation" is saying the obvious: meaning-based translation is, in fact, the only kind of translation possible. (Zukovsky and Zukovsky's [1969] attempts at "phonemic translation" do not involve verbal communication proper, since the semantic properties of the linguistic expression are irrelevant to the intentions of the "translators.")

However, there is one way, at least in principle, by which we can *simulate* a direct quotation from one language to another. Remember that, from a communicative point of view, the most interesting characteristic of a direct quotation is that it gives the target audience potential access to the full original interpretation. We could now make this our basic demand: that we want to produce a stimulus in the target language that will communicate to the target audience the full interpretation of the original, that is, that it will share with the original *all* implications the original author intended to communicate. If we think of interpretive use as a cline or continuum, going from no interpretive resemblance to complete interpretive resemblance, then what we are looking at here is the extreme case of interpretive use, aiming at *complete interpretive resemblance* with the original.

From the condition of communicability that we have already explored, it is immediately clear that the success of any attempt to communicate the original interpretation will require that this target-language stimulus be processed *using the context envisaged by the original author;* otherwise there is no reason to expect that this interpretation will be optimally relevant to the target audience. And without that condition being fulfilled, the audience will not be able to get at the original interpretation. This condition is no different from using a direct quotation within the same language.

Thus, we have, in fact, arrived at a possible absolute definition of translation, which we might call *direct translation* because of its relation to direct quotation: *A receptor-language utterance is a direct translation of a source-language utterance if, and only if, it presumes to interpretively resemble the original completely (in the context envisaged for the original).* There are two reasons why this definition says *"presumes* to interpretively resemble": (1) It seems crucial for translation that the receptor-language text be, in fact, presented as the representation of an original; otherwise there is danger of miscommunication. (2) There is a presumption, not a guarantee, of success.

Notice that this notion of translation is indeed independent of the receptor-language context—it is defined with regard to the original context, no matter who the target audience might be. In terms of relevance theory, this notion of translation would be defined as the extreme of interpretive use, presuming total interpretive resemblance.

Notice, furthermore, that if successful, direct translation would fulfil what has been the dream of many translators and translation theorists: to communicate the full intended interpretation of the original to the target audience. Also, because of the causal relationship between interpretation, stimulus, and context, the target-language text would display the target-language properties that correspond to the source-language properties of the original.

Of course, the big question is, *Can* it be successful? This depends on answers to two further questions: (1) Do the linguistic means of the target language allow the construction of such a stimulus? (2) Is the target audience in a position to use the original context for interpreting the translation?

To the degree that these two questions can be answered in the affirmative for a pair of texts from different languages, such direct translation can be successful.

What we have arrived at now may be summarized as follows: Relevance theory covers the whole range of interlingual interpretive use, from full resemblance to very little or no resemblance at all. In each case communicative success will depend on consistency with the principle of relevance, which comes across as a presumption of faithfulness, that is, as a presumption of close enough resemblance with the original in relevant respects.

We noted two peculiarities of the extreme case of interlingual interpretive use: (1) It simulates a "direct quotation" across languages in that it allows the receptors access to the originally intended interpretation. But (2) it does so only under the condition that the receptors use the contextual assumptions envisaged by the original communicator.

The question now is: Given that we have this wide range of options, what do we do as Bible translators? The answer lies in our understanding the relation between translation and successful communication. To understand this issue, the groundwork will be laid first with a number of key statements.

5.5 Successfully communicating in translation

Let me say very emphatically that these key statements are *meant to be neither exhaustive nor final.* A number of them will no doubt need refinement or modification as we, as translators, try to put them into use. Furthermore, my main aim is not to lay down rules and laws, but to highlight aspects of translation that need more attention than they have been given hitherto.

The first eight key statements concern the overall approach to translation. They are general principles of successful communication in translation.

(1) There are general laws of communication that relate stimulus, context, and interpretation in a cause-effect relation. A translation can achieve its objectives only to the degree that it is in agreement with these laws of communication.

(2) This cause-effect nature of communication means that the first question in translation is not what we *want* to communicate by our translation but what we reasonably *can* communicate. In other words, translators need to address the issue of *communicability* squarely, which has been largely ignored. Normative statements about the objective of translation made in ignorance of this condition are not helpful and only create frustration.

(3) Communicability is crucially dependent on context. What a translation can achieve is only partially determined by what is expressed in the text. A large part, and indeed often the larger part, of the meaning is dependent on the contextual knowledge (or otherwise) of the receptors.

(4) In concrete terms, a translation can communicate the full intended meaning of the original only if the receptor audience has access to the full context envisaged by the original

communicator. Any approach to translation that believes the communication of the full meaning can be achieved by a good translation alone, *regardless of receptor context*, is doomed to failure.

(5) The converse of the last statement is also true. The less the context available to the receptors resembles the context assumed by the original communicator, the less the meaning conveyed by the translation will resemble the original. This limitation holds true regardless of whether the translation is literal, idiomatic, or dynamically equivalent.

Thus, the Dumagat people simply will not grasp the points of Acts 15 or of Hebrew 7 *until they have acquired sufficient biblical background knowledge.* The Tonga people will continue to misunderstand Naomi's emigration until they appreciate that, in the culture of her day, it had nothing to do with witchcraft.

(6) Translations that do not fulfil the requirement of communicability, that is, that prove to be inconsistent with the principle of relevance for the receptors, run a great risk of remaining unread.

This means that translations require not only the provision of the missing historical and sociocultural information of biblical times, but there must also be materials that enable today's readers to see the relevance of the biblical texts to their own lives. (Documentation for the importance of this requirement has been provided, for example, by Wayne Dye's study of Bible Translation Strategy (1980), which we mentioned in an earlier lecture.) Therefore:

(7) It must be clearly recognized that the final objectives of Scripture translation cannot be realized by translation alone.

(8) Translation projects need to be seen in the wider context of communication, rather than book production. In particular, they need to provide strategies that will enable the audience to eventually bridge the contextual gap.

The next set of key statements (9–12) deals with *the contextual gap* and *how it can be bridged.* We tend to think of the contextual gap primarily in terms of differences between the original context and the receptors' context, but there is another level at which contextual assumptions need to match if the translation is to be successful, that is, at the level of translator and the target audience. The intentions of the translator as to what the translation needs to communicate should match what the receptors expect a translation to do;

otherwise there can be serious trouble. While this factor has caused a lot of misunderstandings, unjustified criticism, confusion, and frustration, to my knowledge it has rarely been singled out and addressed as such. Yet in the framework of relevance theory, it can be seen as a crucial factor. Communicator and audience need to share not only contextual assumptions relating to the meaning content of the utterance, but also relating to the nature of the communication act as such.

One of the clearest examples I know of has recently been documented by Dooley (1989) regarding a translation of the New Testament into the Guaraní language of Brazil. A draft translation following the idiomatic approach was completed in 1982 and a number of copies given out to be tested on a limited scale. After a year's testing, the church decided that the translation had to be changed. Dooley reports, "The changes were so extensive that virtually everything had to be translated and keyboarded again" (1989:51). The following guideline could forestall such unfortunate experiences:

(9) Before starting their work, translators need to ensure that what they intend to communicate by the translation matches what the receptors expect from it. These intentions and expectations are an important part of the context in which the communication takes place, and their agreement is crucial for the success of the translation. (This does not prejudge the issue as to whose views should prevail!)

The implementation of this guideline presupposes several things. First it assumes that there is openness on both sides. Yet, unfortunately, I think there has been a strong tendency on the part of translators to decide what kind of translation the receptors should get. Because we ourselves may be convinced that an "idiomatic" model or a "functional equivalence" model (or whatever other model we might adhere to) is the best model of translation there is, we expect the receptors to take our word for it, even though each model has its problems as well as strengths. If we would leave our own normative model aside, we could see that there is legitimate room for discussion and mutually agreed decisions. In many cases we could sit down with the receptors and discuss these matters with them at a level appropriate to their understanding.

Even if it should not be possible to discuss such a matter in the abstract, we probably could explain it by way of examples, presenting several alternative renderings of a given passage and pointing out the advantages and problems of each. We could present one rendering that is more explicit and another less explicit, showing how the more explicit one is easier to understand but expresses information not actually written in the original which, in the longer term, might need to be dropped when people become more and more familiar with the biblical background. Over against that—it could be explained—the less explicit rendering is harder to understand at first, more open to misinterpretation by uninitiated readers, but closer to the original meaning once the readers know more about the Bible.

Looking for consensus in this matter does not mean that we follow just any whim of a receptor-language audience. Rather, both they and we should be constrained by the beliefs we hold about the Bible, its importance and inspirational nature, in short, by the wider contextual assumptions of our Christian faith. These assumptions narrow down the room for arbitrary deviations (and we may need to bring that to the attention of the audience as well).

Once a consensus has been reached about what kind of resemblance the translation should achieve, it may be helpful to document it clearly in terms of *project-specific translation guidelines*. However, there will be many issues, such as the rendering of key terms, that cannot be covered by general guidelines. These need to be discussed one by one. Thus, throughout their work, translators must *monitor* the agreement between their intentions and the receptors' expectations.

(10) By a careful study and comparison of original and receptor context, translators can predict and anticipate areas of both overlap and mismatch between original context and receptor context. This comparative study of context should ideally involve representatives of the anticipated receptor audience. It may be carried out both intuitively and analytically.

(11) Recognition of *areas of overlap* in contextual knowledge can be used to optimize the impact of the translation program.

Statement 11 is a very important consideration. For example, it can affect the order in which books of the Bible are translated and published. The enthusiasm with which the first book is received may have far-reaching consequences for a whole translation program. If the translator starts with a book that is highly relevant in the target culture so that the project begins with a "bestseller," then people will be eagerly waiting for the next book.

This, incidentally, shows that there is a very important place for anthropological studies in the field of translation. Anthropology can be used to enhance the communicative impact of the translation project by helping the translator identify areas and issues of high relevance to the receptors. These then need to be matched up with biblical texts addressing those issues.

Taking advantage of *overlap* in this way is one type of bridging strategy. But other sorts of bridging are required where there are contextual *gaps*:

(12) Recognition of contextual gaps can be used to develop appropriate bridging strategies: explication in the text, study notes, separate background materials, etc. It is not necessarily the translator's task to implement these strategies; however, for the sake of successful communication, *someone* needs to take care of this. Translators do need to be involved to some extent, not only because they are in a unique position to do so, but also because the way they translate will be directly affected.

Such bridging strategies must be understood by the translator because they will make a difference to the translation. For example, the presence or absence of study notes may determine how little or how much information the translator feels compelled to make explicit in the text. Furthermore, one of the best ways of developing study notes is to sketch them in the process of translating. That is the time when the problems are fresh in the translator's mind.

The next several key statements are important guidelines that address the problem of loss of meaning:

(13) In view of the inspired nature of the biblical texts, there seems to be little disagreement that *the aim of Bible translation is, ultimately, to communicate the full intended interpretation of the original*, as far as we have access to it.

It seems reasonable to assume that all Bible translators would subscribe to this objective in principle; none of us is happy with loss of meaning. (It is well worth noting that, in the relevance theory approach, the notion of "full intended interpretation", i.e., complete interpretive resemblance, is not limited to the semantic contents, but includes what other approaches have divided into "emotional meaning," "connotative meaning," "illocutionary force," and so forth. All of these are subsumed by the explicatures and implicatures of the original text.)

The question on which we may differ is: What is the best strategy to achieve this aim? Some of us believe that a certain amount of deviation from the meaning expressed in the original may be called for in order to make it easier to get more of the implicated meaning across to the uninitiated reader. Others are more hesitant about this, feeling that a translation should accurately reflect what the original expressed and how it expressed it. In order to be able to choose between these options—which are extremes on a cline—I propose that we apply guidelines 14 and 15:

(14) Translators should have a firm grasp of hitherto neglected aspects of meaning. In particular, they should understand that there are important differences between expressing and implicating information, between strong and weak communication. They should understand the importance of open-endedness in communication, especially for figurative language and poetic effects, and the danger of limitation and distortion that can arise from explication. Such awareness will provide much sharper tools for discovering the intended meaning of the original in their exegesis and for decision-making in the translation work.

(15) When dealing with translation problems, translators should be encouraged to ensure that they have a clear understanding of the nature and causes of any particular problem. Then they should look for an acceptable solution in line with the agreed translation guidelines and, if necessary, in consultation with the receptor audience.

Guideline 15 will enable translators to distinguish between *genuine translation problems*, due to mismatches in the linguistic resources of the two languages, and *communication problems* due to the mismatches in contextual assumptions between the original audience and the target audience. This distinction is important because the inclusion or explication of contextual information in the text has always a distorting influence, sometimes bigger, sometimes smaller.

For example, even the little additions, like *"people called* Pharisees" and *"river* Jordan," communicate to the reader that the people and places were probably unknown to the original readers, since the writer explained the names to them. In some cases this distortion may, of course, be considered negligible, especially when compared with the problems that uninitiated readers would have *without* these explanations.

In other instances, the distortion may be more noticeable, and translators have felt more reticent to make such explications. Instances of direct speech are a good case in point. I think many translators would think twice before adopting the rendering "Jesus said, 'Woe to you people called Pharisees.' " Such an explicated rendering seems to have a much greater potential for misinterpretation—as if Jesus were objecting in some way to the Pharisees being called "Pharisees"—an implicature we have no reason to be believe was intended in the original.

Indeed, the translator must be aware that explication of implicit meaning—however big or small the explication—always has the potential for distorting the original meaning. Furthermore, there are important long-term perspectives that need to be thought about. First, while explication is obviously advantageous to uninitiated readers, in the long run it will often prejudge a deeper and richer understanding of the originally intended meaning, since it focuses on one particular aspect of meaning, perhaps precluding the reader from exploring wider ramifications of the original intention. Second, once explicated, these renderings become part of the sacred biblical text for the readers, and changes or removals at later stages may cause their own problems, including the charge of a paternalistic attitude on the part of the translator.

The urge to explicate implicit information in the translated text will depend on how narrow or wide an approach is used for communicating the meaning of Scripture. In a narrow approach that builds mainly or almost exclusively on the translated text alone, this urge will be felt more strongly than in a wider approach that anticipates contextual gaps and incorporates additional means for narrowing or closing these gaps.

In view of the general need for a wide approach and of the potential long-term problems explication may create, it seems only reasonable to adopt the general strategy that problems should be tackled at their root. Linguistic problems should be solved by linguistic means, and contextual problems should be solved by helping the receptors build up the necessary contextual knowledge. In this way distorting influences can be minimized in the long term.

There seem to be many instances where translators resort too quickly to something like explication or the change from figurative to nonfigurative renderings without really having understood the problem (see Gutt 1985). Part of the problem here is that structural analyses have often not been adequate to disentangle the complexities of meaning, especially where the interaction between meaning expressed and context is concerned. Therefore:

(16) Translators should understand that unnaturalness arises from inconsistencies with the principle of relevance.

Unnaturalness can be reduced to inconsistency with the principle of relevance. Thus if the translator uses an unusual word or uncommon construction that does not lead to *more* contextual effects than a common word or construction, this requires gratuitous processing effort from the audience and consequently the translator's rendering will be found inconsistent with the principle of relevance.

However, in evaluating naturalness, the influence of the contextual gap should be kept in mind. A rendering may seem unnatural to the receptors not because the translator expressed himself awkwardly, requiring more processing effort than warranted by the contextual effects, but rather because the receptors lack the contextual information required to derive those additional contextual effects. In this case, the translation would be adequate but a way to close the contextual gap should be sought. Hence, *unnaturalness cannot be judged on the basis of receptor intuition alone*—the original interpretation and context need to be taken into consideration. This is an important point to keep in mind when testing the naturalness of translations.

5.6 Summary

Because of the great importance of the biblical text for the historical and spiritual foundations of our Christian faith, I think we all agree that the ultimate aim of Bible translation must be that of communicating the full intended interpretation of the original to the receptors, as far as we have access to that. None of us feel happy about loss of meaning relative to the original.

Where we disagree is how this objective can best be reached. To some of us, the freer rendering seems preferable because measures, such as explication, can help to communicate *more* of the intended meaning of the original than a rendering that more closely represents what was actually expressed in the original.

However, this is not the whole story. As relevance theory helps us see, there are significant differences between expressing information and implicating it. Implicated meaning cannot usually be communicated explicitly without some distortion, for explication often narrows the range of information conveyed and misrepresents the strength with which it was intended to be communicated.

If a translation is viewed from the perspective of context, other differences between freer and stricter translations emerge. Freer translations communicate more of the meaning of the original to receptors *as long as these lack biblical contextual knowledge*. But the more knowledge of the biblical context the receptors acquire, the less helpful the "extra" explicated meaning becomes. In fact, there is a point where the distorting influence of explication prevents users of a freer translation from getting as close to the meaning of the original as users of stricter translations.

Thus, if the receptor audience is progressively acquiring more knowledge of the biblical context, sooner or later the freer translation will keep them from a deeper knowledge of the original meaning. On the other hand, there will no doubt always be new readers coming along who lack this background knowledge, and for them the freer translation will serve well.

Thus we find that the freer translation and the stricter one serve two different audiences: The former is easier for those who have little background; the latter gives a richer meaning to those with more biblical knowledge. However, due to the contextual gap between the original audience and almost any present-day receptors, it seems safe to say that neither type of translation will wholly satisfy the principle of relevance for present-day audiences, at least for significant parts of the biblical text. Therefore, it is an absolutely essential requirement that translations be embedded in a wider framework of communication that closes the relevance gap. Otherwise, we can predict that many translations will remain unread.

BIBLIOGRAPHY

SELECTED BIBLIOGRAPHY ON RELEVANCE THEORY

A. Basic and introductory works

Gutt, Ernst-August. 1986a. Unravelling meaning: An introduction to relevance theory. *Notes on Translation* 112:10–20.
———. 1991. *Translation and relevance: Cognition and context.* Oxford and Cambridge, Mass.: Blackwell.
Smith, Neil V. 1989. *The twitter machine.* Oxford: Blackwell.
Sperber, Dan, and Deirdre Wilson. 1986a, *Relevance: Communication and cognition.* Oxford: Blackwell.
Wilson, Deirdre, and Dan Sperber. 1988a. Representation and relevance. In *Mental representations: The interface between language and reality*, ed. Ruth M. Kempson, 133–53. Cambridge: Cambridge University Press.

B. Advanced, specialized reading

1. Discourse

Blakemore, Diane. 1987. *Semantic constraints on relevance.* Oxford: Blackwell.
———. 1988a. "So" as a constraint on relevance. In *Mental representations: The interface between language and reality*, ed. Ruth M. Kempson, 183–195. Cambridge: Cambridge University Press.
———. 1988b. The organization of discourse. In *Language: The socio-cultural context*, F. J. Newmeyer, ed., vol. 4, 229–50.
Blass, Regina. 1986. Cohesion, coherence and relevance. *Notes on Linguistics* 34:41–64.
———. 1988. Discourse connectivity and constraints on relevance in Sissala. Ph.D. dissertation. University of London.
———. 1989. Pragmatic effects of coordination: The case of "and" in Sissala. In R. Carston (1989), 32–53.
———. 1990. *Relevance relations in discourse: A study with special reference to Sissala.* Cambridge Studies in Linguistics Series. Cambridge: Cambridge University Press.
Carston, Robyn, ed. 1989. *University College London Working Papers in Linguistics*, vol. 1. London: University College.
Gutt, Ernst-August. 1988a. Towards an analysis of pragmatic connectives in Silt'i. *Proceedings of the Eighth International Conference of Ethiopian Studies* (Addis Ababa University), 26–30.
Harris, John, ed. 1990. *University College London Working Papers in Linguistics*, vol. 2. London: University College.
Rouchota, Villy. 1990. But: Contradiction and relevance. J. Harris (1990), 65–81.

2. Figurative language

Furlong, Anne. 1989. Towards an inferential account of metonymy. In R. Carston (1989), 136–45.

Pilkington, Adrian. 1989. Poetic effects: A relevance perspective. In R. Carston (1989), 119–35.

Sperber, Dan, and Deirdre Wilson. 1986b. Loose talk. In *Proceedings of the Aristotelian Society*, vol. 86, 153–71.

Wilson, Deirdre, and Dan Sperber. 1989. On verbal irony. In R. Carston (1989), 96–118.

3. Translation

Gutt, Ernst-August. 1985. Relevance theory and increased accuracy in translation. *Notes on Translation* 107:29–31.

———. 1986b. Matthew 9:4–17 in the light of relevance theory. *Notes on Translation* 113:13–20.

———. 1988b. From translation to effective communication. *Notes on Translation* 2(1):24–40.

———. 1989. Translation and relevance. In R. Carston (1989), 75–95.

———. 1990. A theoretical account of translation—without a translation theory. *Target: International Journal of Translation Studies* 2(2): 135–64.

———. 1991. *Translation and relevance: Cognition and context*. Oxford and Cambridge, Mass.: Blackwell.

4. Tense, mood and aspect

Smith, Neil V. 1990. Observations on the pragmatics of tense. In J. Harris (1990), 82–94.

Wilson, Deirdre, and Dan Sperber. 1988b. Mood and the analysis of non-declarative sentences. In *Human agency: Language, duty and value*, ed. J. Dancy, J. Moravcsik, and C. W. Taylor, 77–101. Stanford: Stanford University Press.

Zegarac, Wladimir. 1990. Pragmatics and verbal aspect. In R. Carston (1989), 103–47.

Zegarac, Wladimir. 1989. Relevance theory and the meaning of the English progressive. In R. Carston (1989), 19–31.

5. Other

Carston, Robyn. 1988a. Implicature, explicature, and truth-theoretic semantics. In *Mental representations: The interface between language and reality*, ed. Ruth M. Kempson, 155–81. Cambridge: Cambridge University Press.

———. 1988b. Language and cognition. In *Linguistics: The Cambridge survey*, vol. 3 of *Language: Psychological and biological aspects*, ed. F. J. Newmeyer, 38–68.. Cambridge: Cambridge University Press.

————. 1990. Quantity maxims and generalized implicature. In J. Harris (1990), 1-31.

Clark, B., and Geoff Lindsey. 1990. Intonation and syntax in non-declaratives: A pragmatic account. In J. Harris (1990), 32-51.

Groefsema, Marjolein. 1989. Relevance: Processing implications. In R. Carston (1989), 146-68.

House, Jill. 1989. The relevance of intonation? In R. Carston (1989), 3-18.

Itani-Kaufmann, Reiko. 1990. Explicature and explicit attitude. In J. Harris (1990), 52-64.

Kempson, Ruth M., ed. 1988. *Mental representations: The interface between language and reality.* Cambridge: Cambridge University Press.

Smith, Neil V. 1989. Can pragmatics fix parameters? In R. Carston (1989), 169-80.

Sperber, Dan, and Deirdre Wilson. 1987. Précis of relevance: Communication and cognition. *Behavioural And Brain Sciences* 10:697-754. (Includes a good collection of reviews of *Relevance: Communication and Cognition*)

Wilson, Deirdre, and Dan Sperber. 1985. An outline of relevance theory. In *Encontro de Linguistas Actas*, Unidade Científico-Pedagógica de Letras e Artes. Universidade do Minho, Minho, Portugal, 21-41.

————. 1990. Linguistic form and relevance. In J. Harris (1990), 95-112.

OTHER WORKS REFERRED TO IN THIS VOLUME

Dooley, Robert A. 1989. Style and acceptability: the Guaraní New Testament. *Notes on Translation* 3(1):49-57.

Dye, Wayne T. 1980. *The Bible translation strategy.* Dallas: Wycliffe Bible Translators.

Headland, Thomas. 1981. Information overload and communication problems in the Casiguran Dumagat New Testament. *Notes on Translation* 83:19-27.

Leach, E. 1976. *Culture and communication.* Cambridge: Cambridge University Press.

Levy, Jirï. 1969. *Die literarisch übersetzung: Theorie einer Kunstgattung.* Frankfurt: Athenäum.

Svejcer, A. D. 1981. Levels of equivalence or translation models? In *Kontrastive Linguistik und über—setzungswissenschaft, Akten des Internationalen Kollequims Trier/Saarbrücken,* ed. W. Külwein, G. Thome, and W. Wills, 320-323. München: Fink.

Wendland, Ernst R. 1987. *The cultural factor in Bible translation: A study of communicating the Word of God in a central African cultural context.* London: United Bible Societies.

Wilss, Wolfram. 1982. *The science of translation: Problems and methods.* Tübingen: Narr.

Zukofsky, Celia, and Louis Zukofsky. 1969. *Catullus.* London.

Printed in November 2022
by Rotomail Italia S.p.A., Vignate (MI) - Italy